BURT FRANKLIN: RESEARCH & SOURCE WORKS SERIES 688
Selected Essays in History, Economics and Social Science 241

OVERPRODUCTION AND CRISES

OVERPRODUCTION AND CRISES

BY

KARL RODBERTUS

TRANSLATED BY

JULIA FRANKLIN

With an Introduction by

JOHN B. CLARK

PROFESSOR OF POLITICAL ECONOMY IN COLUMBIA UNIVERSITY

BURT FRANKLIN
NEW YORK

Published by LENOX HILL Pub. & Dist. Co. (Burt Franklin)
235 East 44th St., New York, N.Y. 10017
Originally Published: 1898
Reprinted: 1971
Printed in the U.S.A.

S.B.N.: 8337-30401
Library of Congress Card Catalog No.: 78-153033
Burt Franklin: Research and Source Works Series 688
Selected Essays in History, Economics and Social Science 241

Reprinted from the original edition in the University of Pennsylvania Library.

INTRODUCTION

BY

PROFESSOR JOHN B. CLARK.

THE modern world regards business crises much as the ancient Egyptians regarded the overflowings of the Nile. The phenomenon recurs at intervals; it is of great importance to every-one, and natural causes of it are not in sight. An economist may make a formula that tells, to his own satisfaction, why a convulsion in business takes place about once in a decade; but if the statement is at all complete, it will hardly be understood by the public. It will necessarily be intricate. The phenomenon is complex, and a statement that accurately accounts for it must be so. The most available reasons that can be assigned for business crises are vaguely expressed in single terms, such as "overproduction," "inflation," "speculation," and "liquidation."

Of the terms that may be used for this purpose, the one that most nearly satisfies the public mind is *overproduction.* It describes what, in the time of a crisis, and in the case of many producers, is a reality, namely, the possession of goods that they have made and cannot sell, except at a ruinous sacrifice. It is, moreover, a true instinct that dictates the resort to this particular explanation. Before every commercial crisis there is a period during which there takes place very much production that does not cater to normal and permanent wants, and that, therefore, cannot continue. Much production needs to be checked, and it is checked by the harsh operation of the crisis itself. The so-called "boom" has deranged business, and the ensuing depression is a time of painful readjustment and recuperation. It is a time of convalescence from the disease that is rudely described as an excess of production, and that really is an excess of some kinds of production and a deficiency of other kinds.

Rodbertus' *Theory of Crises* was published in 1850–51. It has the merit of conforming to the popular instinct. It ascribes crises to overproduction. That universal overproduction is impossible has been considered nearly axiomatic, and certainly it is not possible that more of every kind of article should be created than is wanted by the entire public. If we deal very cavalierly with human nature and with society, we can suppose a case of overproduction like this; but we cannot make it appear possible. We can imagine a society in which men are all alike, and in which they want one unit of each article that is made, and no more. They also want no other kinds of articles. Every man, if he had a second unit of anything that he already possesses, would find it in the way; and if, now, through new machinery, a second unit of everything were to be created, it would clearly be an excess.

In the world of reality we have insatiable wants to deal with, and an unusable surplus of all things can never be produced. An *unsaleable* surplus of *many* things can be produced. Overproduction is practically misdirected production. Rodbertus' own theory of gluts really reduces them to misdirected production, however little his own language and thought may have made such a reduction. We have only to create, in imagination, the condition that Rodbertus describes—that of a society devoting a fixed fraction of its productive power to making goods for labourers, while the labourers are able to buy and pay for a diminishing share of these goods—in order to see that the trouble would be relieved if a certain portion of the productive power were used for making what other classes desire.

The making of a relative excess of some things is, indeed, a real phenomenon of what are called "hard times." If we can detect the actual cause of this misuse of productive energy, we shall go far toward attaining a true philosophy of crises.

Something has misled business men and has made them cater to a demand that is unnatural and transient. If we know just what has done this, we have removed the mystery from the cause of crises. It is doubtless something that falls under the general term, speculation. Future values have been anticipated; men have thought they saw amounts of wealth coming to them that appeared ample. If these had only been real, they would have justified large expenditures in anticipation of them. Orders for large amounts of consumers' wealth have been given, and the mills have been set running in order to meet them.

The goods have come into existence; but the wealth that was seen in a vision of the future has not materialized. The mills have made cloth, shoes, furniture, etc.; and the values that were to have paid for these things have resolved themselves into a mirage.

The critical test of a theory of so-called overproduction, which, in actual fact, is always unbalanced or misdirected production, is whether it refers this phenomenon to a cause that is real, and that actually deludes employers, and makes them run their mills on goods that are not "effectually demanded." A fatuous discounting of the future might do this. It might cause articles to be made for persons who want them, but find that they cannot pay for them. Let men order goods in the expectation of paying for them with wealth that is apparently about to exist. The producers fill the orders that, in such conditions, are given to them. Consumer's delusions result in producer's blunders.

Rodbertus' theory of "overproduction" lacks this particular element. It involves no delusion on the consumers' side. These men go on spending their daily incomes and no more; yet the producers create too much for them. That occurs which cannot occur in a community in which mills are run according to the orders that they get. If what is sold to-day is the basis of what, as may be assumed, will be sold to-morrow, the kind of overproduction of a certain class of goods that is the basis of Rodbertus' theory of crises cannot take place.

Let wage earners get a diminishing fraction of the income of society; let employers make for wage earners goods that shall represent a fixed fraction of the income of society; and a case of misdirected production is presented. There are now too many things of the kinds that only wage earners will use. This is the nature of Rodbertus' assumption.

It makes producers cease to follow the effectual demands of consumers. It makes them run their mills on coarse clothing, heavy shoes, etc., long after the workmen have ceased to buy them. It makes the manufacturers deliberately accumulate an excess of stock in the absence of either a present or a prospective demand for it. There is no delusion on the consumers' part as to what they *can* pay for, and there is no reason for any delusion on the producers' part as to what the consumers *will* pay for. There is a perverse failure to make the actual demand of yesterday a basis for the production of to-day, or to make the demand of last year a basis for the production of this year.

Let wage earners at first get two-thirds of the gross income of society. Two-thirds of the consumers' goods annually created by society will then consist of things that are adapted to the working men's needs. Now let the terms of distribution be so changed that the workmen get only a half of the income of society; and if there are still made goods for these men's use that embody two-thirds of the gross income of society, there is an excess of such goods. One-sixth of the gross income of society is now embodied in goods that will not be bought by the class for which they were intended.

Now the change in the terms of distribution that is the basis of this theory must come about gradually. A slow-acting and general cause is, as is assumed, making wages in the aggregate to constitute a smaller and smaller fraction of the total gains of the world. This is an assumption, indeed, that requires statistical proof; but Rodbertus believed that this proof could be furnished. Even he could not have claimed that the reduction of the relative income of the working class is made suddenly. Slow and permanent must be the changes that would cause wages to shrink relatively, and to constitute a dwindling fraction of the whole income of the world.

In view of the gradual character of this change, what follows? The producers have all the evidence that business men need as to what kinds of products will be effectually demanded. Very sensitive is production to slow changes in consumption, and very efficient is competition in making it to be so. Short would be the business career of an employer, who, after a year or two of shrinking demand for his goods, should continue to make these things in fixed or increasing amounts. No competitor in a business can survive who does not develop a greater capacity than this implies for creating things that the public calls for. Even sudden changes in demand—the capricious actions of fashion—must be and are respected by the mass of successful producers. The spectacle of a great body of employers going serenely on in making for workmen more things than, by reason of some gradual and natural change, workmen can buy, is not one that will bear the test of comparison with facts. Speculations, delusions about the future, and fictitious incomes in the present may bewilder consumers, and, through them, may misdirect producers. Slow changes in the terms of distribution cannot do this.

The theory of crises that Rodbertus advanced furnished the substance of the doctrine on this subject that reappeared in the writings of Marx. The chief conclusion to which the theory leads is that crises are a normal result of a competitive wage system. They result from a steady and permanent change in the terms of distribution, and this change results from a natural law of Wages. The full proof that crises are a necessary part of the economy of society, as now organized, rests, therefore, partly on the theory of Wages; and it is clear that the view of this subject that was held in Rodbertus' time is now held by few economists. Not many men now believe in the Ricardian Iron Law doctrine concerning the earnings of labour. If the productivity theory of Wages is true,—if a natural law tends to give to the worker what he specifically creates, and if that amount is an increasing one—the major premise of Rodbertus' reasoning about crises must be reconsidered. What is of most interest, however, in direct connection with this theory itself, is the deduction that is drawn from the old wages doctrine. Is this deduction legitimate, even on the assumption that the Iron Law theory of Wages is true? Here is a specific weakness that needs only to be stated to be admitted by candid men. Whatever qualities producing employers may lack, they have the capacity to bring the kinds of goods that, from year to year, they make into a general conformity to any gradually changing demand. Fictitious demands—visions of coming wealth on the consumer's side—may baffle them, but a steady and permanent change in the rate of wages cannot do so.

Rodbertus' theory is presented in the form of a controversial letter to his scientific friend, von Kirchmann, who is an acute reasoner and one with whom Rodbertus agrees up to a certain point. Von Kirchmann's statement of the problem, as he conceives it—which is cited at great length by Rodbertus—is admirably clear. Three employers have each three hundred workmen, and with them constitute an isolated community engaged in internal trade. One-half of the product of each establishment goes as wages to the workmen, and the other half remains as the share of the capitalist-employer. To the nine hundred labourers there accrue as wages the products created by four hundred and fifty men.

It is, of course, to be noted that this force of labourers is aided by the machines, materials, etc., furnished by the employers, and that it is a loose use of terms to say that the whole working force gets, as its pay, only the product of a half of the force. What they get is a joint product of one-half of the labour and one-half of the capital in the establishments. Moreover, if the productivity theory of wages is true, these capitalists could not, in the long run, get one-half of the product of their establishments unless, by an accurate tracing of products to their sources, it could be shown that one-half of the product is virtually created by capital and the other half by labour. Instead of saying "Employers get, as their shares, the product of the labour of four hundred and fifty men, aided by capital," we might, with greater clearness, say, "Employers get the product of all the capital; and it amounts to a half of the product of the establishment."

Accepting, however, the form of expression adopted by von Kirchmann, we may create an imaginary case of "overproduction," which clearly resolves itself into misdirected production. The food, coarse clothing, etc., created by the four hundred and fifty men constitute the real wages of the nine hundred. Finer products created by the remaining four hundred and fifty men constitute the real incomes of the three employers.

The employers now take, according to von Kirchmann, the heroic resolution of using, in luxurious consumption, only the labour of one hundred men, and of devoting to the building of new mills, etc., the labour of three hundred and fifty. They "save" seven-ninths of their incomes and "spend" two-ninths. This amounts to taking the larger fraction of their gains in a different concrete form from that in which they take the smaller fraction. Having at their command the services of four hundred and fifty men, they dictate what these men shall make, and take it as their real incomes. They take mills instead of luxuries as the chief part of their returns.

The problem of determining what happens as the sequel of this decision is arithmetical and not difficult, though at first it appears slightly puzzling. According to von Kirchmann, the new mills at first make coarse products, of the kinds that workmen use. As one-half of the labouring population is already engaged in making such things, and as the whole labouring population cannot have more than the product of this half, the situation ensures a glut of coarse products. If, on the other hand, the new mills are set running on luxuries they create a glut of these things; for the employers already use, in this form, the product of one hundred men, and they have heroically resolved never to use more than that.

The reader will see that the logical difficulty vanishes if we state in different terms what the resolution of the employers really signifies. It means that they determine to take in the form of additions to their productive plants, not only the products of the three hundred and fifty men, but the entire future products created by those additional plants themselves. They definitely restrict their own future personal consumption to the product of one hundred men. Nature restricts the consumption of the nine hundred labourers to the product created by four hundred and fifty. Five hundred and fifty men work to create consumers' goods; and the reason why the remainder of the force is not so occupied is that the employers demand, as the result of all further agencies at their command, nothing but additions to the working plant, which is their capital. The employers' heroic abstinence means that the new capital shall compound itself for ever. The new mills, farms, etc., shall create more mills, farms, etc. If they do this, the case still presents no glut.

The importance of the problem justifies any amount of attention that may be required for the solving of what is really a logical puzzle connected with it. The key to the solution lies in recognizing the unquestionable fact that saving is in reality demanding and getting productive instruments as a part of an income. If capitalists were, like the three employers in von Kirchmann's illustration, resolved to save all of their incomes, present and future, beyond a fixed amount, they would capitalize, first, a part of their present means, and then all later income from the capital so created. They would build mills that should make more mills for ever.

This case presents no glut; but it is an unreal case. What the three supposed employers do is unlike what actual capitalists always do. The rich men of the world of reality make no such heroic and perverse resolution to take as consumers' goods and use in their own consumption only a fixed amount of wealth. As their incomes increase their consumption increases with them. They "save" something—which means that they keep men working to make productive plants—and they "spend" something—which means that they keep other men working on consumers' goods. In the two ways they keep in employment all the men whose services they command. The labourers themselves keep in employment the remainder of the working force.

Every mill that is built means, naturally, a new income for its owner. This income causes an increased demand for luxuries, and goods of these higher grades can all the while be made and sold. Production does not need to try to over-feed and over-clothe the poor for lack of other consumers to cater to. While the mills are building, the surplus productive energies of society are used in building them; and when the mills are running, these energies are largely used in catering to the higher wants of the owners, to whom the mills have secured new incomes.

Let a manufacturer extend his plant, and let a farmer drain a swamp and bring it into cultivation. Both have new incomes, and both require for their consumption goods of finer qualities. The manufacturer will make finer cloth for the farmer, and the farmer will raise finer vegetables and more fruit for the manufacturer. Moreover, the creation of these new productive plants gives to labour itself a larger wealth-creating power, and raises wages. There are finer goods now to be made for the labourers themselves. A steady turning of the productive energies of society into new channels, a gradual diversion of more power to the making of luxuries, is the consequence of such an increase in productive machinery. There is no need of crises because of such a steady change and improvement. Let the mills turn out food and coarse goods for labourers, and luxuries and also more mills for the capitalists, and the problem is solved; but incidental to this solution—which is the actual one reached in the practical world—is a steady improvement in the quality of the goods that are received and used by the labourers. The new mills mean rising wages. Von Kirchmann's case of over-abstinence on employers' part does not involve business convulsions; it does involve prosperity for workmen. Rodbertus' theory of the relative fall in wages, as compared with the total social income, does not call for crises. The difficulty is removed by giving to each class its real income in the concrete forms in which it demands it. This is something that employers are compelled by competition to accomplish; and they do it in a nearly perfect manner. It is in the relations of present to future—in speculative and inaccurate estimates of incomes that are about to be—that there lie influences that cause goods to be created for which, in time, there is no effectual demand.

As the earliest well-known attempt to connect crises with overproduction, and that with a law of Distribution, this work of Rodbertus is of great scientific interest. If it had asserted that crises are due to misdirected production, it would have stated an essential fact, and it would have remained only to identify the causes of the misdirection.

Miss Franklin has put the English-reading public under much obligation by this excellent translation of an economic classic. She and her readers are to be congratulated on the success that she has had in overcoming the difficulties of Rodbertus' style, and in giving to the reader something that is accurate as a translation and clear as an English statement of a subtle theory. The book will furnish as useful an introduction as a student can have to the theory of crises.

JOHN B. CLARK.

COLUMBIA UNIVERSITY,
NEW YORK.

OVERPRODUCTION AND CRISES

YOU, like myself, my honoured friend, recognize that it is pauperism and a glutted market that lie at the root of the economic distresses of the time; and no one, I should think, who has sufficiently reflected upon the subject, can fail to perceive this. It is, then, in our views of the causes and remedies only that we find ourselves differing from others. I shall first give a complete account of the investigation of the *causes*, according to your conception of them as well as mine, before proceeding to a consideration of the remedies proposed by you and by myself, for the counteraction of them.

You, like so many others, do not trace those phenomena back to one single cause, *to one single error* in the present economic organization. You agree with me, indeed, in the conviction that they spring from *economic* circumstances and relations, while so many—merely from lack of thorough comprehension of political economy—account for them on social grounds of a general nature, or even on moral grounds; but you assign a different economic circumstance as the cause of pauperism, and still other economic circumstances as the cause of gluts.

You have devoted to the explanation of these two phenomena two dissertations, *Die Grundrente in socialer Beziehung* and *Die Tauschgesellschaft*.

In the first of these you account for *pauperism* on the basis of the fundamental law which, according to Ricardo, governs the creation and increase of the rent of land. You fully agree with him upon his theory of rent, but do not coincide in all the inferences which that famous man has deduced from it. You draw other conclusions from it, conclusions which ought by all means to follow from it, if—if, indeed, the theory itself were a correct one. I must take the privilege of quoting from my paper, to which you also make reference, "An Inquiry concerning Present Economic Conditions," in which already I called attention to the fact that Ricardo's method was not logical. The passage is as follows:—

"Ricardo has a different view of the fall of profit, and McCulloch shares his view, inasmuch as he understands by profit the *relative* share of the capitalist in the product. Since both let rent arise in its own special way, they put the share in the product contained therein to one side, and then let the other two shares in the product, wages and profit, vary inversely to each other. They hold accordingly, that in consequence of the increasing unproductiveness of the land, and because the [real] wages of labour consist in the main of the products of the soil, wages in their nominal amount and consequently also as relative share in the product, become continually greater, and for this reason the relative share of the capitalist in the product, *i.e.*, profit, becomes continually smaller.

"Yet even admitting the hypothesis of the increasing unproductiveness of the soil, that theory is wrong. Of course, if the effect which rent has upon profit is once for all considered as having already been taken into account, and is thenceforward left out of the discussion, a change in the profit on capital can take place only in the case of an inverse change in wages. But then that would be the most trivial of propositions. The real question is, what is the fundamental law which governs the constant fall of profit on capital? One must not, therefore, leave out of account one share in the product, and consider only the inverse changes in the other two, but specially investigate *which one* of the different shares chiefly effects, by its changes, the fall of profit on capital. This fall, however, is due far more, even according to the Ricardian view of rent and of the increasing unproductiveness of agriculture, to rent than to wages. For if by the rise in value of raw material wages are relatively increased, then the relative share of the land-owner must increase still more, because this is affected *solely* by the price of raw materials, while wages involve another factor besides the labour of producing raw materials—the ever-increasingly productive processes of manufacture and of transportation. One cannot, therefore, consider the rise of wages—due to the increasing unproductiveness of the soil—and the consequent fall of profit on capital, without bearing in mind that there occurs *at the same time*, and to a still greater degree, a rise in rent and also a consequent fall in the profit on capital. Ricardo seems to overlook the fact that if poorer soil is brought under cultivation, and the product of good soil rises in value equally with that of the poorer, the landowner's *whole* relative share of the national income must necessarily rise, and that this rise can occur only at the expense of the capitalists' share, as according to his own assumption the labourer's share is increased also."

This conclusion, my honoured friend, which I have deduced in the above extract, and which Ricardo failed to infer, you, for your part, have actually drawn. You also rightly conclude—assuming as true the actually false hypothesis of the increasing unproductiveness of land—that since, on account of the advanced price at which the one new bushel of grain is brought to market, the price of the millions of bushels hitherto raised must rise as well, there must be always less and less of the national product left for wages and profit for the labourer and the capitalist. You also deviate from Ricardo in a second conclusion, namely, you do not allow that wages rise with the rise of the price of grain, but hold that they are maintained at a steady rate or even lowered by certain circumstances of social development. Out of these deviations from the doctrines of your great predecessor you have, while adhering to his principle of rent, constructed for yourself a new theory of pauperism, which appears all the more seductive from your singularly happy manner of presenting it.

I now go on to give an account of this theory by means of extracts from your presentation.

You distinguish a two-fold origin of rent, a historic and an economic one; the former you find in slavery, and the latter in those circumstances from which Ricardo also derives rent. For, you say, "the historic restriction of the labourer to the bare necessaries of life"—to the food of slaves, which leaves remaining a part of the product for rent—"should have disappeared when, at least in Western Europe, the freedom of the person and of occupation were developed, when labourers were no longer obliged to submit to the dictate: 'So much only shall you consume, and the rest deliver to me, your master.' Nevertheless, rent remained, nay, it has even arisen in the populous states of North America, which enjoy complete civil and political liberty. In this case the basis must be a different one, and Ricardo has shown what it is."

According to this, "rent is based upon three circumstances:—

(1) "That no country possesses land and soil of uniform composition or quality, but that they present the most varied degrees of fertility. To this is added the greater proximity or remoteness of the fields from the places where the consumers

live; the location, which increases or diminishes the cost of transportation, has the same effect as difference in fertility.

(2) "That in populous countries the better and nearer land no longer suffices to furnish the amount of raw material required for the nourishment and clothing of the inhabitants, and that therefore poorer and more remote land must be brought into requisition.

(3) "That the price of grain, meat, skins, and all other products of the soil must be uniform for products of the same kind and quality, whether the individual bag of grain be raised upon good or upon poor soil."

For "with the rise in price"—you say in another place—"which is caused by the increase of population and the consequent necessity of cultivating poorer land, the price of the grain grown on good land is, naturally, also raised, and the advantage thereby gained accrues—for the same reason as remarked above, namely, that labour and interest on capital cannot stand at different levels—not to the labourer or the capitalist but to the landowner."

"Let us assume," you continue, "that an acre of good land has hitherto yielded 8 bushels of grain; that the price of a bushel was 1 thlr., and that capitalists and labourers divided these 8 thlrs. among themselves alone. The increase of population necessitates the cultivation of poorer soil which, applying an equal amount of labour and capital, yields only 6 bushels; now it is clear that this grain cannot be sold for less than $1\frac{1}{3}$ thlr. a bushel, because the labourer and capitalist want to get 8 thlr. here as well. But then the price of those bushels grown on good soil rises also; those 8 bushels now cost, at $1\frac{1}{3}$ thlr. per bushel, $10\frac{2}{3}$ thlr., and it is clear that the landowner will in this case too give up only 8 thlr. to the labourer and capitalist, retaining, therefore, $2\frac{2}{3}$ thlr. per acre as rent for himself.

"If the growth of population compels the use of still poorer soil, which yields only 4 bushels, then the price of a bushel of grain must rise to 2 thlr.; although the landlord obtains no rent as yet from this class of soil, he does now from the second class; his rent from the first class now amounts to 8 thlr., from the second to 4 thlr., altogether 12 thlr., while before it amounted to only $2\frac{2}{3}$ thlr.

"The data furnished by experienced agriculturists agree exactly with this view. According to Block's estimates, page 30, the net product from soils of various classes was as follows:—

Class	I. 40–50 per cent. of the gross product of				10 bu.
„	IV. 36–41	„	„	„	7 „
„	VII. 28–38	„	„	„	4 „
„	Xa. 22–32	„	„	„	1 „
„	Xb. 20–30	„	„	„	½ „

"That is to say, that upon good soil the cost of the capital and labour required to obtain 10 bushels of grain amounted to only 4 to 5 bushels, but in order to raise 10 bushels of grain upon poor soil (Xb) 7 to 8 bushels must be expended. In the first, out of 10 bushels 5 to 6 are left over for the landowner as rent, in the last only 2 to 3 bushels."

This principle is, according to you, the most important cause of the increase of rent. "Society," you say, "has hitherto needed 200 million bushels of grain for its maintenance; society has, however, by the blessing of God and the skill of the physician, increased by 100,000 souls. It requires, therefore, the addition of another million bushels of grain to those 200 million. This new million bushels must be raised upon poorer soil, or with a larger outlay of capital, than those 200 million; they cost, therefore, a proportionately greater amount of capital and labour. Those cost 1 thlr. a bushel, these cost 1 thlr. 5 sgr. Society would assuredly be glad to pay this increase of 500,000 silbergroschen, equal to 16,666 thlr. But the land-owner says, 'No! not only these last 100,000 bushels, which alone cost more, shall have this higher price, society shall pay as high for the old 200 million bushels; instead of 16,000 thlr., it shall give us $33\frac{1}{2}$ million thlr. additional'; and society obediently fulfils the command."

"This law," you go on to say, "is not nullified by the progress made in husbandry and by free trade in grain." This, you say, is demonstrated by experience. "These two facts are well known: that the price of grain is constantly, even if slowly, rising, and that these prices, in countries of a pretty equal degree of fertility, are highest where the population is densest. For instance, the average price of rye in Brunswick for fifty-year periods was as follows:—

1500–1550 . .	3.3 markgroschen.
1551–1600 . .	11.6 „
1601–1650 . .	15.9 „
1651–1700 . .	17.1 „
1701–1750 . .	22.5 „
1751–1800 . .	27.5 „

"In Brussels the averages for wheat were:—

1701–1749 . .	57.8 Brabant sols.
1750–1799 . .	68.4 „ „
1800–1849 . .	105.0 „ „

"The experience of all countries furnishes the same result. The sudden jump in the sixteenth century, it is true, is explained by the decline of the value of silver consequent on the discovery of America; but the steady increase is a proof that prices, and therefore rent, increased with the increase of population, in spite of all the improvements in agriculture. The relation in which the average price of rye in Prussia, from the year 1816 to the year 1837, stands to the population in the separate provinces is as follows:—

Province.	Price of Rye.		Population to the square mile in 1837.
Prussia . . .	32.2 sgr.	...	1827 souls.
Posen . . .	34.3 „	...	2180 „
Brandenburg and Pomerania	38.4 „	...	2093 „
Saxony . . .	40.3 „	...	3396 „
Silesia . . .	38.0 „	...	3612 „
Westphalia . . .	47.75 „	...	3600 „
Rhine Province . .	49.4 „	...	5078 „

(Compare RAU'S *Political Economy*, page 226.)

"In Wurtemburg we have the following relations:—

District.	Average Rent of an Acre.		Population to the square mile.
Danube . .	3.96 fl.	...	3300 souls.
Jaxt . .	3.42 „	...	3600 „
Black Forest .	4.0 „	...	4800 „
Neckar . .	5.7 „	...	7200 „

"We see here that prices keep almost exact pace with density of population, and the slight deviations in the first table may be readily accounted for by the greater productivity of Silesia and the greater difficulty it has, as compared with Saxony, in finding a market. If it were possible to increase productivity in husbandry in like proportion with the increase in population, why does not this increase take place on the Rhine, where the price—more than half again as high—certainly strongly incites and urges the agriculturist to it?"

"It is evident," you continue, "that the improvements in agriculture have at all events contributed to check the excessive rise of prices and thus of rent; but it is also evident that they are not able fully to counteract the law; and we may look forward to a time when this law will be far more powerfully manifested, especially in Prussia, namely, when the separations and the peasantry regulations will have been consummated, whereby the chief obstacle to agricultural productivity and industry will have been removed, but at the same time this great source of increase of productivity will have been exhausted."

In this law which governs rent, and accordingly

in rent itself, as it is actually created and increased, you see the cause of the growing impoverishment of society. You argue: since population is constantly increasing, not, indeed, as Malthus holds, in proportion to the food supply, but rather, on the contrary, in proportion to the scarcity of that supply and the wretchedness of the population; and since, moreover, wages do not, as Ricardo holds, rise in equal proportion with the rise in rent; the share of the three classes—the labourer, the capitalist, and the landowner—in the product gets shifted by the rise in rent, in spite of the increased productivity in all branches of industry; the shares of the first two classes are diminished in favour of the third. Rent is constantly rising in kind and in money, while wages and interest, reckoned by raw materials, are constantly falling. While genius and application augment productivity in all branches of industry, while all classes should enjoy a flow of prosperity, it is the landowner who interposes an ever-growing dam to this stream of happiness. It is natural that it is not the labourer only, but the capitalist also, who suffers by this. The great capitalist, however, with his large income, does not feel this; the small artisan and the labourer, on the other hand, live a life in which the main part of their income is spent on food. The small artisan spends three-fourths of his yearly income for potatoes, bread, butter, oil, and fuel, and only a quarter for clothing, dwelling, and little, simple, social pleasures. This disproportion is still greater in the case of the labourer. He expends seven-eighths of his wages upon food and fuel. What does it avail this class, which comprises seven-eighths of the nation, that the price of calico, cloths, sugar and coffee, knives and scissors is lowered, while that of potatoes, grain, wood, oil, leather is constantly rising? The little that is gained in the purchase of clothing is far from counterbalancing the increased rate of food products; their only recourse is to dress worse than before, live in worse dwellings, and eat less and worse food. Hence the misery of these poor mechanics and of the labourers.

"This is the explanation," you conclude, "of one of the weightiest and most far-reaching phenomena of present society. Notwithstanding that the nation has been freed from its shackles of slavery and hereditary subjection, the labouring classes of the population are materially still for the most part in the old depressed condition. They have been given the right to freedom, but the means wherewith to enjoy this freedom the landlord reserves now, as he did before, to himself, and this supremacy of the landlord is the more dreadful, as it is based upon the apparently unalterable laws of nature and of trade.

"So long as human society cannot abolish the inequalities in the fertility and location of land, the increase of population, and the payment of like prices for like products, so long will it have to suffer the rent of the landowner; so long will the greater part of the fruit of labour have to be delivered over into the hands of a strange master, who, with his hands folded in idleness, permits the labourer to make use of kind Nature's productive forces. But not satisfied with this, every increase in population will only serve to multiply the landowner's share of food products, wood, metals, rent of dwellings, all without his expending any labour. The more children the poor have, the greater the demand of a growing population for work, the smaller will be the share left over for the work of the hungering labourer, and the greater the share that falls into the landowner's pocket; and all this will happen upon the ground of those inexorable laws of nature and of trade, which, like blind Fate, pour riches where they already abound, and rob poverty already suffering from lack of the necessaries of life. Ireland offers an awful instance of this increase of rent, one that must with mathematical certainty be developed in every country having a rapidly growing population, unless, as in England, it is tempered by a great expansion of manufacturing industries. It is rent alone which is the source of the dreadful destitution of Ireland, not the splitting up of the land. For give the farmer the rent he pays, often amounting to £8 for an acre of potato land, and he will be able to return to a decent mode of life, and thus also to restrain the excessive growth of population; for it is only where man in his wretchedness sinks to the level of a brute that this excess of population springs up—a grim and awful contrast of misery and fertility.

"Take, on the other hand, the United States of North America. Its prosperity, its strength, lies simply and alone in the fact that rents do not as yet exist in the greater part of the Union, and are, in the remaining portions, very low. The rate of interest and the rate of wages are both, as is well known, very high in America; the usual rate of interest is from eight to twelve per cent.; the daily wages of a labourer, one dollar and above.

But what would this high rate of interest and of wages avail if rents stood in the proportion in which they do in Western Germany? It is well known that wages and the rate of profit are the factors which determine the price of all goods, including the products of the soil; these last because those produced upon the poorest soil set the price, and yet yield no rent. Now, when interest and wages are high, the price of all products is high also; the labourer gains nothing in consequence; his wages are three times as high, but so also are bread, cloth, the rent of his dwelling, light, and wood three times as dear, and thus he can procure no more indulgences for himself than before. This result would be literally verified in America were the rents the same as in Germany. But the superabundance of fertile soil relatively to the present population, together with their excellent and cheap means of transportation, enable them to raise sixteen bushels on an acre, whereas, with the same amount of capital and labour applied to the last grade of land, we should, here in Germany, produce perhaps two bushels. Though the rate of interest and of wages be, therefore, three times as great as in Germany, their returns from the soil are eight times as great, and consequently the price of corn three-eighths of the price in Germany. This holds good, of course, of all products of the earth, as well as of corn; that is why meat, leather, and all raw materials are also only half as dear as in Germany. Now, since in such products as cloth and shoes a great part of the value consists in the raw material, it follows that these products, too, in spite of the high wages and interest, can be manufactured lower than in Germany. Those goods alone form an exception where the work required to transform the raw material is very great—articles of luxury, and those demanding skill, which, therefore, are lower in Germany than in America.

"Thus a labourer in North America who does not require luxuries is six times as well off as one in Germany, solely because rent is either low or does not as yet exist at all. His wages are three times as great and the prices of all his necessaries only half as high as in Germany. He can eat more meat every day, drink more beer, and, if he chooses, need not work as much as does a very well-to-do mechanic and citizen with us.

"That this fortunate condition of the population of North America is based solely upon the fact that they are either totally exempt from rent or that the rents are very low, can never be too deeply impressed upon the mind or too often repeated. All other grounds upon which it is customary to account for it are either deceptive, or merely skim the surface of the reality, or turn upon hazy notions, such as 'virgin soil,' 'a rising nation,' which are but a cloak to ignorance.

"Ireland and North America: these are the antipodes in the effects of rent. There, wretchedness and men lowered to the state of brutes; here, prosperity, activity, stirring, happy life everywhere.

"Germany's position is between the two; but towards which one is it tending? Towards the conditions prevailing in Ireland, or towards those in America? To one who understands the state of society the answer cannot long remain doubtful. The tendency is a downward one, towards the misery of Ireland. It is beyond doubt that in Germany, too, and particularly in Prussia, rents are regularly rising; all the miseries, therefore, attendant upon an excessive increase in rent the future, though it may be only a distant one, holds in store for our country also, should the present conditions continue."

While in this first treatise you trace pauperism

back to this one cause—the presumed law of rent—in the second you find the explanation of gluts in a mass of circumstances, so to say in the whole character of present-day traffic. I shall give a faithful abstract of this theory also.

You put as the brunt of your argument: "that the greatest part of the social evils spring not from deficient production, but from a deficient market for products; that the more a country is able to produce, the more means it possesses of satisfying all its needs, the greater is the danger it incurs of being exposed to misery and want."

This question of a market affects the capitalist as well as the merchant, the agriculturist as well as the mechanic; even "the much-vexed question of the right to work finally resolves itself into a question of how to find a market."

"We see"—you conclude therefore—"that the social problem is almost identical with the problem of a market. The evils of that so much abused competition even disappear with the certainty of a market; its good features alone would remain; the emulation to provide good and cheap wares; but the life-and-death struggle which is caused solely by the want of a market will disappear."

You then proceed to give Say's explanation of

a market, which may be expressed in these words: Products are bought only with products—production, therefore, constitutes its own market—and where on one side there appears to be an overproduction, there is, on the other, but too little. You show how these propositions, universal as their truth may be, "do not exhaust the actual facts," and add: "There are still other laws hidden in trade which prevent the clear working of those propositions, and it is by their discovery alone that the present glut in the markets can be explained; and by this discovery, too, perhaps, a means may be found to obviate this great evil. We believe that there are three circumstances in the present system of society which cause the contradictions between Say's indubitable law and the actual state of things.

"These circumstances are: (1) the too unequal distribution of products among those who have contributed to their creation; (2) the difficulties, either constant and enduring, or changing and unequal, which Nature interposes in the production of raw materials; (3) the inadequacy and defectiveness of the present system of trade, that is, of the agency which acts as a medium between production and consumption."

A closer examination of these circumstances forms the principal matter of this, your second treatise.

"The first circumstance"—to use your own words—may be more concisely expressed by saying "that wages are too low, that from this cause arises stagnation in trade. To one who understands that the two factors which alone regulate the price of goods are wages and rate of profit, this proposition may appear strange; if wages are low, so also is the price of goods low; if, again, the former are high, the latter, too, will be high. Wages and prices, then, are in a direct proportion and compensate each other. The only reason that England abolished its duty on corn, as well as on meat and other articles of food, was in order to lower the working-man's wages, and thus enable the manufacturer to drive out all other competitors in the markets of the world by still cheaper goods. This view is correct, however, only in part, and does not touch upon the proportion, which here is the only thing to be considered, the proportion in which production is divided between capital and labour. The too unequal distribution between these two is the first and weightiest reason why Say's law is not actually realized; why, in spite of production in every branch, all the markets suffer from over-supply. This assertion is so important that it demands an exact proof. Let us assume, to simplify the proof, that the inhabitants of a certain place supply all their own wants by their own production; that this production consists of three kinds only: one supplies the clothing; the second, food, light, and fuel; and the third, dwellings, furniture, and implements. In each one of these departments of production there is an *entrepreneur* who furnishes the capital and the raw material, and 300 workmen who do the mechanical part of the work. The result in each one of these departments is that the workman receives as his wages one-half of the yearly products, and that the *entrepreneur* gets the other half as interest on his capital and profit on his undertaking.

"This place, then, consists of 903 inhabitants, who themselves produce all their necessaries; the one who undertakes to provide the clothing for these 903 inhabitants is very able to do so with his body of 300 workmen; and so can he who is to furnish food, light, and fuel very well succeed, with his 300 labourers, in obtaining the requisite food and materials for all the 903 people from the cultivation of the soil; the same is true of the one who undertakes to provide dwellings and implements; he can, with his 300 workmen, furnish the repairs, the new constructions, as well as the furniture, housekeeping utensils, and all the implements needed for dwelling and housekeeping purposes for the 903 inhabitants. This locality, then, possesses all the conditions requisite to secure a general well-being for all its inhabitants. All, accordingly, start out fresh and full of courage to their work. But after a few days the matter appears in quite a different aspect; those 900 workmen have only the very scantiest clothing, food, and dwelling-places, and those three *entrepreneurs* have their warehouses filled with clothes and raw materials, and houses standing vacant; they complain of the lack of a market, and the workmen, on the contrary, of their inability to satisfy their wants, just as is the case in actual life to-day. How does this happen in a place where the forces and means of production are so justly employed and apportioned that, taking all the inhabitants and their wants into consideration, nothing could be better? We see that in this place the trouble does not lie, as Say and Rau hold, in the fact that too much is produced in one branch of industry and too little in another, or that there is a deficiency in the aggregate means of production. No. The means are just so great, their apportionment to the different industries just so arranged, that all of the 903 inhabitants could procure for themselves good and ample clothing and nourishment, and good and ample dwellings. That, in spite of all, this does not take place, that there is an obstruction, is due simply and solely to the way the products are divided; the distribution is not an equal one among all, for the *entrepreneurs* retain as interest and profit half for themselves and give only half to the workmen. It is clear that the man engaged in working on clothes, therefore, can get in exchange for half of his productions only half of the products required for nourishment, dwelling, and so on, and it is clear that the *entrepreneurs* cannot get rid of the other half, because none of the workmen have any products left to exchange with him. The *entrepreneurs* are lost with their abundance, the workmen with their hunger and their nakedness.

"The unequal distribution which is the cause of this condition of simultaneous superfluity and misery, is but another name for wages and profit.

"The misery of this village, then, is caused solely by the fact that the *entrepreneur* does not share equally with his workmen; that is, that he appropriates a part of the products beforehand—before the distribution takes place. If he divided equally, without such deduction, every man engaged in making clothes would be able to obtain his own clothing with one-third of his product, exchange his second third for food, fuel, and light, and, using his remaining third as rent, procure for himself a healthy and comfortable dwelling. The workmen in the other two branches of production would be in the same position, and *all the inhabitants* of the village comfortable and happy; they would be plentifully nourished and clothed, and have good dwellings, without having to work one moment longer than where the *entrepreneur* retains half as his profit. We have in this village a mathematical demonstration that Say's law does not suffice; that the marketing of products through products alone cannot be secured; that there enters, rather, another element, which is concerned with the distribution of products among those who have contributed to create them."

You find this fundamental example applicable to the great commercial intercourse of the real world, because the circumstances that "instead of three kinds of production there are a hundred and more in actual society"; that "the proportion in which the *entrepreneurs* share with the workmen is not always a half, but, it may be, a third or a fourth"; that "the *entrepreneurs* do not own a capital with which they conduct business"; that "in reality production in the various branches is not so abundant that all members could, with an equal division, obtain ample satisfaction for their wants"; that "wages and profit are paid not in kind, but in money"—all these circumstances would not in any essential particular alter the force of that example.

"There are, however," you continue, "two points of difference between our village and the real world, which may exert greater influence than those hitherto mentioned; these are luxury and foreign trade, which, in connection with this question, stand in close relation to each other.

"In our fictitious locality the *entrepreneurs* found their stock accumulating because they could not themselves make use of the entire half of the total production of clothing, food, dwellings, and household materials, which fell to their share as profit, and because the 900 workmen had not the means to purchase it of them. Now, it may be said that this surplus would at once disappear if half of the workmen, instead of making such ordinary goods, would manufacture articles of luxury, which require more capital and labour; those 450 workmen would, in consequence, produce no more goods than the *entrepreneurs* can consume. It is in the nature of luxuries that they enable the consumer to utilize more of the producing power of capital and labour than is possible in the case of ordinary goods.

"Should the three *entrepreneurs* agree to these propositions the state of things would be as follows: instead of 300 workmen there would be but 150 employed in making clothing; these would still be able to manufacture as much clothing as the entire population used before; it is the surplus of clothing only which would be eliminated by taking away 150 of the men from the work on clothing—a surplus which the *entrepreneurs* had hitherto retained as profit, and which accumulated because they could not consume the profit in this shape themselves. The *entrepreneur*, consequently, decides to employ these 150 and the same amount of capital with which these men had worked before upon the manufacture of articles of luxury. He employs them, for instance, in making fine embroidery, elegant laces, costly shawls, and handsome carriages. Conducting his enterprise in this manner the *entrepreneur* thus obtains, instead of a surplus of ordinary clothes, just the quantity of rich clothing, cloths, carriages, and so on, that the three *entrepreneurs* of the place can conveniently make use of themselves. The wages which he is to pay these 150 workmen, engaged in manufacturing luxuries, he gets from the clothing which the other 150 workmen are obliged now, as before, to deliver up to him.

"Should the second and third *entrepreneur* proceed in a like manner, the 900 workmen would continue to live in the same penury as before; the three *entrepreneurs*, however, would, in consequence of having luxuries produced instead of limiting themselves to the manufacture of ordinary goods, be relieved of the embarrassment of having to live in an inferior style while masses of unsaleable goods lay heaped up around them; they would themselves be able to consume the products which the 450 men working on articles of luxury now produce, and thus avoid altogether the piling up of unsaleable wares."

Now we find, of course, luxury existing on a

great scale in real life also; yet, you ask with good reason, Why, in spite of the most refined luxury, is there a glut of all kinds of products, common and expensive alike?

"The only answer possible is that this glut of goods in the real world is due solely to the fact that there is too little luxury, or, in other words, *that as yet too little is consumed by the capitalists; that is, by those who have the means of consumption.*"

This assertion, which you yourself acknowledge is a glaring contradiction of the now prevailing views of political economy, according to which saving is the primary condition of the welfare of nations, you proceed to prove in the following manner. You revert to that fundamental example in which you showed that the *luxury* of the three *entrepreneurs* obviated over-production, and continue: "Now let us suppose a case, one commended in political economy as preferable, a case of productive consumption. In this case the *entrepreneurs* say: We do not wish to consume our income down to the last penny in luxury and show; we shall use it again in productive investments. What does that mean? It means nothing but the founding of new productive enterprises of all kinds, by means of which commodities will again be obtained; the sale of these commodities is to furnish the interest on the unconsumed capital of the three *entrepreneurs* which they have saved and invested. The three *entrepreneurs* determine, accordingly, to consume the production of 100 workmen only; that is, to materially retrench their luxuries, and to employ the labour-power of the remaining 350 men, and the capital they had used, in the founding of new productive enterprises. But now the question arises, In what departments of industry should this capital be invested? The three *entrepreneurs* have the choice only of starting either manufactories of ordinary goods, or manufactories of luxuries. They choose at first the former. The first year is devoted to setting up the new factories; constructing workshops for tailors, shoemakers, and so forth; preparing the new ground for grain and raw products; establishing new quarries for building houses; constructing new machines for the manufacture of household implements and utensils. The second year, the arrangements being completed, the 350 men are employed in producing the new commodities. But the three *entrepreneurs* soon notice with dismay that they are confronted with the same difficulty as in the first instance; for there is no one who could purchase their stock of them. The 900 workmen, in consequence of their scant pay, are only able to buy the products of the 450 workmen who have continued in their old industries; that which the 350 additional men have now produced, much as they would like to consume it, much as they may feel the need for it, is beyond their reach; they have no means to buy it. Neither would the three *entrepreneurs* buy it of each other, for they cannot consume these ordinary goods themselves.

"In angry mood the three *entrepreneurs* now turn their productive consumption, their investment of new capital, in the other direction. No places are fitted up for the manufacture of ordinary goods, only those for the manufacture of luxuries. All the arrangements and appliances are completed by the first year; the second, they proceed to the work. At the end of this year the *entrepreneurs* are astonished to see that they have by this means only reverted to the second case; for there is no one to purchase these luxuries from them, unless they should buy them of each other; and this they do not wish to do because they desire to save and not to consume, and the 100 workmen suffice to secure them moderate comfort. Thus we see that in the simple conditions of this place it is by no means possible for this so-called productive consumption, of which political economists make so much, to ameliorate the condition of society, to promote its progress. The population is always confronted with this dilemma: The three *entrepreneurs* must either expend their income to the last penny in comforts and luxuries of every description, in which case all the 900 workmen will at least be able to make a living, even though a miserable one, or if they curtail their luxuries and determine to save, they find no market, the goods accumulate, and part of the workmen will have no work and therefore no means of subsistence."

It is the same, you maintain, in real life. "It is because capitalists consume too little unproductively and too much productively," that in spite of the prevalence of luxury we still in actual life have deficient markets, accumulation of goods, and lack of opportunity for labour. The enormous accumulation of capital in recent times is, according to you, the cause of these evils. The real world—you hold—finds itself in the same dilemma as the village in our oft-quoted example.

"The accumulation of capital does not, as is well known, consist in the mere storing up of goods, or in the heaping up of quantities of money and bullion to lie unused in the owner's cellar; whoever wishes to save does so by investing his savings—either himself or through others—profitably as capital, and thus deriving an income from them. Such income is only possible if this capital is employed in such new enterprises as are capable of yielding the required interest. One man builds a ship, another builds a barn, the third cultivates a barren heath with his savings, the fourth gets himself a new spinning-jenny, the fifth buys more leather and engages more journeymen, in order to extend his shoemaker's trade—and so on. Only in thus applying it will the capital that has been saved bear interest, which is the end and aim of all saving.

"Now, in real life, as well as in our imagined community, even before this new accumulation of capital, seven-eighths of the inhabitants—that is, all those who live by the products of their labour, the mechanic who works in a small way, the small landed proprietor—were unable to buy more than the barest necessaries, the things they had been consuming all along; and the remaining eighth, although able, had not the desire to buy more, because their overruling tendency is to save.

"What, then, is to become of those new commodities which are produced by the new capital invested in the form of ships, machinery, improvement of land, and which serve to furnish the interest? If they are ordinary goods the well-to-do (the last one-eighth) do not wish them, and the poor—the first seven-eighths—cannot buy them, for they do not earn any more than before; the former amount of products amply sufficed to furnish what they could afford to purchase. If, on the contrary, they are luxuries, the poor, naturally, are still less able to buy them; the rich, of course, could do so, but on account of the predominant tendency to save before mentioned, they will not. It is then quite inevitable that this predominant tendency of modern times, to save, must produce gluts in the markets, and as a consequence augment want in the labouring class.

"The condition of all manufacturing countries is the most convincing proof of this; all the warehouses are full, everybody is intently, eagerly seeking a market, and the majority want to save, that is, to increase the amount of commodities still more, and by that means augment their fortune and their income."

You believe that the objections of political economy to this view spring from delusion and short-sightedness. In the first place it overlooks the fact that this amassing of goods certainly does not at once follow the new accumulation of capital. The fitting up of places for business, the transformation of money-capital into really productive capital, the consequently increasing demands at first manifested for the various products and also for work, blind the eyes of political economy. "As soon, however, as the machines are set in motion, as soon as the new products are sent to the markets, the occupation of the men engaged in fitting out the enterprises ceases, and the capitalist is now anxious to dispose of his wares; but in vain does he look around for a purchaser. The number and the circumstances of the consumers have remained totally unchanged; the former arrangements for producing commodities were adequate to supply their wants, and no one is able to buy the new increase." According to your opinion, the political economists are right only so far as regards the beginnings of the new application of capital. In order that those enterprises should secure the working-men permanent employment, a market must in addition be found for the increased quantity of goods; but with the system of wages hitherto prevailing "the labourers have no means with which to purchase." We must, of course, you say, distinguish between the two directions taken by accumulations of capital. Part is applied to new inventions. New applications of capital of this kind indisputably prove most beneficial to society as a whole, for they yield cheaper and better wares, the labourer can better satisfy his wants "with unchanged money-wages"; but in *exchange value* he cannot consume any more than before; and his gain in the enhanced *quality* and *usefulness* of his commodities does not lessen the glut in the markets, because the increased productiveness has augmented the quantity in a like proportion. But even this species of application of capital depresses wages because it takes away work from the labourer; and even should this be the case only in the beginning of the undertaking, Proudhon is right when he says that, as inventions never cease, this beginning never ends.

"But," you add, "the second sort of new application of capital consists in the multiplication of enterprises in the old lines; consequently new artisans engage in business, new factories are set up, new ships built, the flocks of sheep increased, and so on. It is clear that this second sort of capital-accumulation must necessarily increase the piling up of stock, the glut in the market. For it does not, as has been shown, have the effect of raising wages; more goods, merely of the old familiar kinds are produced at the old rates, and no one can or no one wishes to buy them, for reasons so often stated."

You therefore regard the enormous accumulations of capital in recent times as advantageous only to society as a whole, not to the individual. For when the calm observer looks upon those nations so rich in capital, he sees with astonishment on turning his attention to the individual, who hitherto has appeared to him only as a part of a great whole, that in spite of these enormous accumulations of capital, in spite of the countless inventions for the guidance and mastery of the forces of nature and of man, but a small part of the resulting advantages are enjoyed by all branches of society; that the greater part of these advantages accrue to the benefit of a chosen class only, and that, owing to the hitherto prevailing system of wages and profit, and to the tendency to save, these fortunate classes themselves occupy a paradoxical position which allows them no rest. Selfishness impels them to take from the labourer in the shape of interest on capital and *entrepreneurs'* profit, half of the product and his ability to consume; and from selfishness again they themselves refrain from consuming, while with a blind eagerness they continue to set up new establishments of production to produce things that no one can buy. Seated in the midst of all the means of enjoyment, they can neither make up their minds to let the labourers standing around them reap the benefits, nor to make use of them themselves. Like another Sisyphus, they torment themselves with an insoluble contradiction—a desire to sell, after they have deprived the buyer of the means wherewith to buy. Present-day society may, indeed, be well compared to a band of travellers in the desert. Suffering with thirst, they find a spring which would suffice to refresh and strengthen them all; but a small number constitute themselves masters of the spring; they grudge giving the majority more than a few drops to quench their thirst; they themselves take long draughts, but the stream flows faster than they are able to drink, and so from satiety and want of goodwill they let half of the gushing stream waste itself in the sand.

Neither can an increase of population, according to you, prevent these results caused by the accumulation of capital. If it be in proportion to the latter, it produces no change in the hitherto existing glut; if the accumulation of capital is in the lead, the glut becomes still greater; if, again, population increases at the greater rate, the glut would not cease, only the misery of the poor would be increased, because the additional number of labourers would in that case find no employment on account of lack of capital; the glut remains the same, while the starvation of these new labourers is added besides.

Nor does foreign trade, in your opinion, create any change in this disconsolate state of things; for the essence of this trade is either "to increase the variety of goods in the home market" or to increase productivity. "Either, then," you conclude, "these goods which foreign trade through its factories offers the nation for sale are common, in which case the capitalist *does not wish* to buy them, and the labourer cannot do so because he has not the means, or they are luxuries, in which case the labourer is, naturally, still *less able* to buy them, and the capitalist, owing to his endeavour to save, does not want them."

You believe that by the foregoing arguments you have set forth the *first* of those three circumstances to which you charge the existence of gluts, namely, the too unequal distribution of products among those who have contributed to create them. You say repeatedly that society cannot consume the fruits of its enormous masses of capital, because the labourer's share of the product is too small. I have had to follow you pretty fully in this portion of your treatise, partly in order to give a just idea of your peculiar conception of the nature and effects of capital, partly because I do not agree with you in a single one of the grounds upon which you derive gluts from the disproportionate division of products. Your views upon the other two circumstances I shall be able to extract more briefly.

"Agriculture differs essentially," you say, "from all other productive industries in two points: in the very unequal crops, varying as they do with the fruitfulness of the year, though the amount of capital and labour expended remain the same, and in the ever-increasing difficulty, in the populous countries of Europe, of augmenting the average quantity of the products of the soil."

The first peculiarity has, according to you, only an indirect effect upon the markets. From the fluctuations in the market price of food products it results that the farmer class receives now so many millions more and again just so many millions less. Though, therefore, consumption "remains, on the whole, the same *in value*, it does not *in kind*. But with this change in the kind of consumption a change must also be made in the kinds of production, and the necessary consequence is that all productive industries are affected, and now flourish, now languish, according to the varying price of grain."

But the second peculiarity of agriculture has, according to you, a direct effect upon the problem of markets. "In the industrial countries of Europe all the good or well-situated land has," you assert, "long since been brought under cultivation, and all the improvements have been effected which bear promise of yielding revenue; that is, the current rate of interest on the outlay. Credit, which, through the institution of the mortgage, is pre-eminently at the landowner's command, the long-continued peace, and the abundance of capital before the era of railroad-building, necessarily led to this result. Excepting, then, unfortunate individual cases, individual neglected estates, agriculture has for the last twenty years been in such a condition that new investments of capital, whether they be employed in opening up new soil or in improving the old, no longer yield the current rate of interest, at the prices which agricultural products now command. Only when the population increases and the consequent demand makes the increase in prices a permanent one will a new application of capital be made possible."

But the increase of population, you say, is slow, its effect is markedly noticeable only after the lapse of decades, while other circumstances may convert the rise of prices into a fall. Thus the repeal of the English corn laws lowered the price of grain in Prussia also for a considerable time. Prussia lost, thereby, a great deal on its export trade to England. With the former sliding scale of duties those countries alone which lay close to England could engage in the business of exporting grain to that country—this closeness enabling them to take rapid advantage of the fluctuations in the duty, which often lasted only a few weeks. Since the imposition of a fixed duty of one shilling (equal to 10 sgr.) per quarter (equal to $3\frac{1}{2}$ Berlin bushels) all countries, even the most remote, are able to carry on a regular traffic in grain with England; and it is well known what immense quantities of flour North America has since then been sending there. Prussia will never again, in spite of an almost nominal duty, reach its former height of grain exports to England, and, therefore, until this former English consumption is made up by an increased population at home the price in Prussia must fall.

The reason, you believe, that during longer or shorter periods of time the greatest of all industries—agriculture—does not permit of any new investments of capital is because it does not yield the current rate of interest; "the necessary consequence, therefore, is that the newly-saved capital, especially that amassed in agriculture, is applied almost exclusively to commerce, manufactures, and the various trades; and thus the gluts, arising from causes above explained, are still further increased." Another injurious effect which this presumed increasing agricultural unproductiveness is supposed to have upon the markets is that while on the one hand it restricts the application of capital to husbandry, on the other, through the rise in rent which it entails, it lessens the labourer's and artisan's ability to purchase.

The *third* circumstance, finally, which you mention as the cause of gluts, consists in the nature of modern commerce and the part that money plays in it.

Hitherto traffic has been considered without this intermediate factor. Things, however, you say, are not bought with products, but with money. "The producing of anything engenders a desire to buy; this is undoubtedly true, but the desire is of no avail if the power to fulfil it is lacking; and it is only money that gives this power; that is, one's own productions must be sold—converted into money. Money has, therefore, assumed for the producer a significance far above its exchange value. The manufacturing and mercantile classes have given the strongest expression to this in their conception of bankruptcy. The goods which a manufacturer has in his warerooms may by far exceed in value the amount of his debts; a banker may have in his desk, against his liabilities, double their amount in notes and public securities; both, nevertheless, are bankrupts in the eyes of the mercantile world if they cannot pay their notes in *cash* the day they fall due.

"Money is the commodity that can buy all others; no other commodity can do this. The capacity to consume, the ability to buy, is, therefore, only half attained by the possession of products; the other equally essential condition is that these products be first *sold*. This second condition offers far more difficulties, these times, than the first, and it is this point that Say has overlooked.

"In a society where sales could be readily effected, where the present disproportion of working-men's wages did not exist, the difficulties in the way of the second condition would, of course, disappear.

"But in a society like that of our modern states, where the consumption of products is already checked by the interest demanded for capital, by rent and the consequent restriction of wages, Say's idea of forcing a market and consumption by an increase of products is an entirely perverted one. Every such increase must augment the pressure for selling, which is the second before-mentioned condition, and thereby magnify the difficulty of selling, of converting products into money.

"Money, therefore, has in our time become the watchword of every manufacturer, every producer, every merchant. In times and in countries where sales are effected with ease and regularity money does not possess a predominating value, and serves merely to facilitate exchange; in times, however, when it is difficult to find a market, the value and effective power of money are raised to an abnormal height, which in its turn exerts an injurious effect upon the markets. The manufacturer cannot with his finished goods pay his workmen or those who supply him with raw material, nor pay for repairs on his machines and buildings; in modern society he can use money only for these purposes; this money he must have at a *fixed time;* in no case may the money be lacking beyond that period if he is to keep his business free from ruinous interruptions and himself from bankruptcy. But the sale of his goods, by which means he wants to obtain the money, does not rest with him; events of the most various nature may intervene to check this sale. Yet the sale must be effected by a certain time in order that the money due at that time should be on hand, and thus this pressure creates that competition, that rush after buyers and a market which in the end serves only to ruin even the regular channels of sale.

"To this danger," you go on to say, "which is primarily caused by the wild struggle for a market of the great and small manufacturers and merchants is added another, the enormous increase of credit to which modern trade has been driven. It is true that in olden times, too, the manufacturer and the wholesale merchant sold to the retail dealer on credit, upon drafts which fell due at the next fair (*Messe*), but his capital was so large that he could keep these drafts in his portfolio until the day they fell due. In the old times it was considered a disgrace not to do so. Nowadays no manufacturer, no merchant, retains his drafts in that manner; he sends them, immediately after acceptance, to the bank to be discounted; that is, he sells these drafts at once, and is thus naturally able to carry on an equally large business with much smaller capital than in the old times. Now the whole system of manufactures and commerce being so arranged that the minimum of capital possible to carry it on is used, it cannot stand even the slightest hitch if the machinery is to be kept going. In olden times capital was larger, and a portion of it remained unused, failure to pay could be better and longer borne; now this is impossible. Out of one hundred business houses ninety-nine cannot now subsist if their drafts are not paid and their products sold by a certain day. The modern age has by most ingenious devices, such as the discounting of notes, the full development of the banking business, achieved for trade something like what it has done for manufactures by the introduction of machines; trade, the exchange of goods, can in consequence be carried on with much less capital than formerly, but this restriction to what is absolutely necessary, though it has contributed essentially to the increase of trade, has at the same time put it into a feverish condition, into a state of tension, such that any disturbance, even a very slight one, shatters the whole structure!"

To recapitulate in brief, your view of the causes of pauperism and gluts is as follows:—

As regards *pauperism*, agriculture, which furnishes material for all industries and nourishment for the human stomach, is always growing more *unproductive;* it requires, according to you, always more labour and capital to satisfy the increasing wants of a growing population. Hence the constant rise in the price of the necessaries of life; hence also a rise in rent, even of land that is worked with no more labour and capital than before; hence constant diminution of the capitalists' and labourers' share; hence *pauperism* among all those classes of people that spend the greatest part of their income upon the necessaries of life.

As regards *commercial crises* they cannot, in your estimation, be traced to an equally simple cause. They are rather the result of three "circumstances" acting together, the first of which consists in the proportion in which products are divided between capitalists and labourers; the second, in the inherent peculiarities of husbandry; and the third, in the present system of money and credit transactions. The ratio of division between capitalists and labourers allows the first too much and the second too little. To the capitalists' excessive share is added their exaggerated bent for saving. Thus capital accumulates and production increases without there being a sufficient number of purchasers for the products, for the capitalists do *not wish* to consume more and the workmen are *not able* to do so. The *second* circumstance, the peculiarity of husbandry, aggravates this first cause of a congested market. Agriculture, by its frequent changes—changes beyond the control of man—of good and bad harvests, fluctuates between high and low prices, and is thus always disturbing the regularity of the markets, the rural population having now much and now little means at their disposal. The increasing unproductivity of the soil exerts a still more direct effect upon gluts. For while, on the one hand, those classes whose income is expended chiefly upon the necessaries of life, are constantly growing less able to buy manufactured products, on the other, the investment of capital in agriculture is rendered more difficult, and what is saved in its pursuit is likewise diverted into manufacturing channels. As, finally, in the *third* place, most enterprises are conducted upon credit, and therefore need money at a "fixed time," there arises a general pressure to sell, which adds another factor to the difficulty of finding a market.

Facts and laws of a nature opposite to what you think you have discovered in history, in statistics, in political economy, and in agriculture, have led me, my honoured friend, to adopt an almost opposite view of the cause of the economic distresses of the time.

I, for my part, find that the Ricardian theory of rent is fundamentally false, and very far from offering an explanation of the social significance of rent. Altogether, I find that all the theories hitherto advanced have failed to make clear the social significance either of rent or of profit, or even of wages. I find that science has as yet shed but little light upon the three branches of national income *in their relation as shares of the product;* also that the peculiar effects of land and capital ownership upon "production and distribution" are as good as ignored. I find also that these laws of the production and distribution of the national product, as influenced by the ownership of land and capital, must be grasped in their connection, in order to obtain access to the cause of commercial crises and of pauperism.

In opposition to your theory, therefore, and to the theories of others, I maintain one which, I assert, is but the consistent sequel of the proposition introduced into the science by Smith and placed upon a still deeper foundation by the school of Ricardo, the proposition that all commodities *economically considered must be regarded solely as the product of labour, as costing nothing but labour* —a proposition of which already Kraus said that it signifies for social science what the unit introduced by Galileo does for velocity in physics.

According to this theory, pauperism and commercial crises spring from *one and the same* cause, it is one and the same circumstance of our present economic system which is answerable for these, the two greatest obstacles to the uniform and uninterrupted progress of society. This circumstance is *that when the distribution of the national product is left to itself, certain circumstances connected with the development of society produce this effect:* **that with increasing productiveness of the labour of society, the wages of the labouring classes become an ever smaller portion of the national product.**

I wish you to understand me clearly. I do not speak of the *quantity* of wages, of the *amount* of bread, meat, stuff which those wages procure the labourer, but of his *relative share* of the product. If, for instance, 100,000 labourers produced 10 million bushels of grain 50 years ago, but to-day produce 20 million bushels, and if each labourer should nevertheless receive to-day, as he did 50 years ago, only 50 bushels as wages, the wages of labour would remain the same in quantity; but as quota, as relative share of the product, they would sink to half of what they were before. They would sink still lower if the quantity, too, should be diminished, say, to 40 bushels, and the quota of product would sink even though the quantity should rise to from 60 to 80 bushels. As share of the product, they would only then not fall, but be maintained, if in quantity they were increased in direct proportion with the increase of productiveness — if they increased from 50 to 100 bushels; because then only would they, as well after as before the increase in productiveness, amount to half of the gross product. I consider it Ricardo's greatest merit to have been the first to advance this conception of the *relative wages of labour*, though, unfortunately, neither his friends nor his opponents knew what to do with it, and Ricardo himself made a perverted use of it; so absorbed was he in his theory of rent, and in the contemplation of the increasing unproductiveness of land, that he even thought that wages as quota of product were constantly *increasing*.

You will grant, my honoured friend, that if it were indeed possible to establish the circumstance that wages to-day are becoming an always smaller share of product, its connection with pauperism and commercial crises would be manifest. For it would appear clear that thereby the labouring classes are excluded from all increase of the national wealth, and, in opposition to the progressively growing income of the other classes, at best only maintain their former income, which, in the present legal and political status of the labouring classes, must, upon economic as well as social grounds, bear pauperism in its train. It would be equally clear that on account of that circumstance the main channel of sale of internal and consequently of the entire national trade, that is, the purchasing power of four-fifths or five-sixths of society, does not expand in proportion to the progressive production, but rather simultaneously contracts in like proportion, from which it would be just as easy to demonstrate the necessity of gluts. I, for my part, am in fact convinced that this circumstance can be shown to exist; I am convinced that in present economic conditions it even asserts itself so strongly that the wages of labour, regarded as quota of product, *fall* in a proportion at least equal to the *rise* of the productiveness of labour, if not in a greater proportion.

The proof that this is so depends evidently upon the proof of two necessary suppositions. It must be shown, first, that productiveness of labour has increased and continues to increase, and, secondly, that the quantitative sum of wages has at best not increased in like proportion, has perhaps remained stationary, or even fallen. Should these two historical preliminaries be demonstrated, the existence of that circumstance must follow as a theoretical conclusion; the fall of wages, as quota of product, *must* then stand in some relation to the increase of productiveness.

It seems, then, that I should only have to undertake the proof of these two suppositions, in order to proceed to the easier demonstration that it is from them that pauperism and commercial crises spring. And yet, I have not reached that point! You, honoured friend, with your knowledge of the present state of economic theory, know best how many concepts still obscure, how many scientific prejudices stand in the way of the very starting-point of this conception of mine. Why, even the idea itself that wages are to be regarded as share of the product is disputed! How different is the general view of the nature and constitution of profit from that which forms the basis of my conception of it! How greatly does the prevailing doctrine of the origin and increase of rent stand in its way! Nay, I do not go too far if I assert that the entire method of treatment to which our science has thus far been subjected makes difficult the comprehension of that proposition to which I trace the economic distresses of our time.

Instead of the science starting out, as it ought to have done, by recognizing that, through the division of labour, society becomes an indissoluble whole; instead of taking, as it should have done, this whole as a starting-point and from it proceeding to explain the separate economic concepts and phenomena; instead, therefore, of placing the idea of national property (the property of society), national production, national capital, national income, and its division into rent, profit, and wages, at the head, and, through these social concepts, explaining the shares of the individual in them, political economy has been unable to escape the exaggerated individualistic tendencies of the time. It has torn into shreds that which, through the division of labour, is an indissoluble whole, a social entity, that which can have being only upon the assumption of the existence of such a whole; and from the shreds, from the particular shares of individuals, it has wished to rise to the conception of the whole. It has, for example, used the property of the individual as a basis, without considering that the property of a person united to other members of society by the division of labour is a thing entirely different from the property of an individual totally isolated, managing for himself. It has started out, for instance, from the rent of a single owner of land, without considering that the conception of rent presupposes that of profit and of wages; that, indeed, none of these conceptions can enter into the discussion unless we presuppose the whole present constitution of society and social income, of which the rent, etc., arising in society are but the *parts*. It has proceeded as if society were but a sum of different economic units, a mathematical and not a moral entity, as if even political economy itself were but an aggregate of individual economies and not an organic combined economy, whose separate organs may be still suffering from the pressure of many a historic circumstance, even from such as partly stand in the way of the rights of the individual also.

Had political economy not fallen into this radically false method it would by this time have assumed a different shape, and certainly have progressed further in its development. I cannot refrain from giving here a brief sketch of a system of political economy such as a method governed by the principle of this science—the division of labour—would demand; more particularly as I am convinced that this sketch will contribute greatly to the understanding of the discussion I have undertaken.

Had political economy sought to follow a right method, it should certainly in a first part of the science, corresponding to the present conception of economics — as a mere natural science of economic intercourse—have started out with the present economic condition of the world, with all the wealth of phenomena it presents, and *its manifestations when left to itself.*

And it should in a *first division* of this part have started out directly from the conception of *national* (social) labour and of the *national* property —the former as the combined action of the individual forces indissolubly bound together into one whole through the division of labour; the latter, as the aggregate of the material goods of the nation, bound together just as indissolubly through the employment of the national labour. Then it should have shown how the circumstance of the division of labour, in the case of every article, breaks up social labour into production-divisions —extractive industry, manufactures, transportation —and these divisions again into production-groups, into individual enterprises; wherefore the national property also is correspondingly subdivided. It should, in the national *property*, have distinguished between national *land*—the more or less abundant source of all materials—and the national *capital*, *i.e.*, the aggregate of the products distributed in various undertakings for use in further productive work; and then it should have set over against the *national capital* the result of the varying national production in a given period of time, *i.e.*, the *national product*. It should have further been shown how one portion of the latter is always destined to be used for *replacing* the capital consumed or impaired in the process of production, and the other portion, the *national income*, for satisfying the direct needs of society and its members. It would then have had to discuss the concept of *national productiveness* and to show therefrom how the magnitude of the national product (and accordingly also of the national income) relatively to the population, in other words, how the *national wealth* depends upon the degree of productiveness.

After such a general exposition of economic conceptions and of their connection with each other, it would have remained to show how the *management* and the *movement* of national production, as well as the distribution of the *national product*, are dependent upon the institutions of positive law.

In order to make clearer the explanation of this dependence upon the most prominent institutions of the positive law of *to-day*, the ownership of land and capital, it should first of all have been shown how different a form the *management and movement of national production* would assume and how necessarily different the *distribution of the national product* would be if land and capital, instead of being private property, were in the possession of society at large, and the *right of property attached only to the share of the national income which each one would receive.* It would not be necessary that under such a condition of things the distribution of the national income should be made according to communistic principles—without laws regulating distributive rights; the measure of everyone's due share could be fixed in accordance with the measure of his work by the legal ordinances of society. The individual labours of workmen, varied as may be their strength and skill, can very well be compared with each other and their relative value estimated. Property, then, under such a condition of things, would not disappear, but only be reduced strictly to its proper and original principle. And there can be no doubt that an economic organization of national production, as well as of distribution of the national product conformable to such a state of the law, could be carried out. The only question would be the practical one, whether the moral strength of the people would be great enough to cause them to persist, of their own free will, upon the path of national *labour*, that is, of national *progress*, without being, as they are to-day, held fast to it, or even driven forward by the scourge of necessity, through the compelling force of land and capital ownership.

It should have been shown by the method of comparison how under a condition of law in which land and capital were social possessions and the national income alone were private property, there would have to be a *public authority* which would undertake to direct the national production in accordance with national needs, or, in other words, to regulate the application of the national property in the most advantageous manner, while under present conditions where the national property is, by the institution of land and capital ownership, divided up among private owners, *the interest of these owners* takes the place of such an authority; these owners likewise applying those parts of the national property which now belong to them, to the production of things intended to meet the needs of society.

It should have been shown how under *those* conditions it would only be necessary for that public authority to issue an order, to bring about the transportation of goods in process of production and still in the public possession, from one production - division and production - locality to another, and at last to its destination, the home of the consumer; while under *these*, where the ownership of land and of capital includes also the ownership of the property produced directly by them, in place of such an order there necessarily intervene, besides the like economic work of transportation, also the *legal business of the sale or exchange of products*, trade and with it money; so that to-day the movement of national production, from beginning to end, *i.e.*, from the first stroke of work applied to the raw material up to the completion of the product, is carried on by a series of property transfers effected through the medium of money.

It would have been necessary to point out how *there* it would devolve upon that public authority to take care that one part of the national production should always be devoted to replacing the capital which has been consumed or impaired in the process of production, and only the remaining portion be used for producing the national income, *i.e.*, the products required to satisfy social needs; while *here*, in place of that care, these things are governed by the management and the interest of the owners of capital or their representatives, the *entrepreneurs*, who regard as profit, as income, that only which trade in their products leaves as a remainder over and above the restitution of capital, and who will undertake such production alone as yields such a remainder.

After having in this manner shown the effect which positive law has upon the *management and movement of production*, its influence upon the *distribution of the national product* would have had to be explained.

It would have been necessary to show how in a state of things in which land and capital belong to society and the national income alone becomes private property, distributed by a principle of justice according to the work rendered, the entire national income would fall to the share of the producers, the workers, while in a state of things in which land and capital ownership exist this income is distributed in such a manner between the labourers, the owners of land, and the owners of capital, that the larger part falls to the last two; how the distribution *there*, where it would be in accordance with the work rendered, would have to be made in such a way that the value of every product would be determined by the time expended upon its production*; and every participant in the national production would receive along with the certificate attesting the time he expended on his work a draft upon an equal value of any desired income-commodities, which commodities would then, after he had given up his draft, be delivered to him from the storehouses of the State, and be considered private property as strictly as are the wages which the workman receives to-day; while *here*, where a division is made between the labourers, the owners of land, and the owners of capital, this division assumes *such* a shape that it is the landowners and the capitalists, or their representatives,

* The constituted value of Proudhon. I must permit myself the remark that the idea of the constituted value was advanced by me before Proudhon, and that the papers in my work *Zur Erkenntniss unserer staatswirtschaftlichen Zustände* contain nothing but the preliminary investigations necessary for the development of that idea.

the *entrepreneurs,* who engage the workmen in production, under a law which governs wages and depresses them far below the value of the product; they then convert the completed product into money, in accordance with the definite value set upon it by the natural laws governing competition and the market; after deducting those wages and replacing the capital (see above) the landowners and the capitalists divide the remaining amount of product under the name of rent and profit among themselves, in accordance with a law founded upon the value of the respective products (raw materials and manufactured products); divide it in order to purchase, just as the workman does with his wages, their share of the national income out of the stores of the various private establishments.

It should, finally, have been shown in the first division of this first part of political economy how it is the distribution of the national income—the magnitude of the individual share—which, in the succession and varying degrees of all human needs, dictates the direction and variety of national production; so that under the one set of conditions the public authority which regulated the kinds of production would have to carry out, just as under the other set of conditions the interest of the landowners and the capitalists does carry out, the mandate contained in this distribution of the national income.

While in this *first* division the economic movement would have been discussed under the presumption of *unchanged* productive forces, in the second the effect of a change in productive forces upon this movement—and the effect, indeed, of a change in the *aggregate* of productive forces as well as of *productivity*—would have had to be exhibited.

In this connection the meaning of *increase of the national capital* and of "*saving*" should first of all have been explained. From this it would have appeared that "saving" is only a form of increase of capital which is dependent upon the existence of land and capital ownership, and whose place can be largely supplied by credit.

It would then have been necessary to show that the increase of the aggregate of the productive forces, consequent upon increased national labour or increased population, is indeed capable of augmenting the national capital and the national product, and therefore revenue* in general and the

* The word *revenue* is used throughout, in what follows, as a technical term to correspond to the author's "*Rente.*" By this

combined national wages; but that this augmentation effects a *rise* [of rate] only in the rent of land, since the increased amount of wages must be distributed among a greater number of labourers, the increased profits of capital be reckoned upon the increased capital invested, and the increased rent of land alone is reckoned upon an unchanged area of land; and that an increase of the *national wealth,* an increase of the national product which might redound to the benefit of *all,* can only occur in case of the increased fruitfulness of labour, increased *productivity.*

Here it should have been shown from what small beginnings national wealth had its rise, how revenue itself—rent of land and profits of capital—was made possible only by the progress of productiveness.

It would further have been necessary to explain, how in a condition in which land and capital ownership did not exist, the result of increased productiveness would accrue solely to the benefit of the labourers, so that their income would increase in direct proportion to the increase of productiveness; while to-day

term he designates generically the income of capitalists, *entrepreneurs*, and landowners, as distinguished from that of labourers.—*Translator*.

that institution, with its law governing wages, has the effect of throwing all the benefits arising from increased productiveness exclusively into the hands of the landowners and the capitalists.

In a *third division*, finally, the question of how to satisfy the needs arising through the existence of society as such and through its "government" would have had to be discussed—and, therefore, in this third division the management of finances or the principles of taxation, and the application of taxes as regards the effect of that application both upon the movement of production and the distribution of the national product, should have been discussed.

After having explained in such a **first part** of political economy "the production, distribution, and consumption of goods," one would naturally have been led to point out in a **second part** the dangers which threaten society if its economic development under existing legal institutions should continue to be *left to itself;* and would finally, in a **third part**, have suggested measures whereby these dangers might be counteracted.

Such a method would carry its own justification with it, even though, regarded strictly, it should as little deserve to be termed *systematic* as that superficial linking together of economic matter, of which Say's school and the Germans have in particular been guilty. But if this latter procedure has contributed to divert attention from the living development of political economy, that method would have made it evident that it is the very fact of political economy now passing through such a living, urgent phase of development, which does not allow its actual problems to assume that symmetry which would permit them to be ranged and classified, like, for instance, those of jurisprudence. That method would at the same time contain an indication that political economy would be capable of systematic treatment and classification only after having passed this phase, and would then become the foremost and most comprehensive of all the social sciences, having in great part absorbed jurisprudence itself.

Had this method been followed in economics, had economists thus proceeded from the whole of society to the individual, the science would to-day contain a far less number of prejudices; the more general recognition of that circumstance which I regard as the cause of pauperism and of commercial crises would have found the ground better prepared for it; I should, in fact, have been able to proceed at once, in order to establish my views, to the proof of the actual increase of the productiveness of labour and the unchanged (or even decreased) wages, and to deduce from the fact of this decrease in wages regarded as *share of the product* the inevitableness of those visitations. As it is, I am obliged to add to the foregoing sketch of a better method a complete theory, in accordance with that better method. They will make each other mutually clearer.

I wish to sum up this new theory, which I place over against the hitherto prevailing one, in a number of propositions which I shall endeavour to make as concise and as clear as possible.

(1) I repeat that wages, interest, rent of land, profits of capital are *social* facts and concepts, *i.e.*, facts and concepts which exist only because the individuals who participate in them are joined by the division of labour into a society; that from the very start one sets out from a false standpoint if one attempts to explain the *principles* which underlie those facts from considerations referring to the *individual* participants, from the standpoint of one of the many labourers, and so on; that one must, on the contrary, in an explanation of principles understand by wages, interest, and so forth

the aggregate wages accruing in the society, or think of the whole of the society as represented by one labourer, one landowner, and one capitalist. For the laws which regulate the further distribution of wages, rent, and profit among the *individual* labourers, the *individual* landowners and the *individual* capitalists are different from the laws which in the first place govern the division of the product into wages, rent, and profit; and in taking the former for the latter economists only continue to do what the Say school has pre-eminently done: to mistake the chance circumstances which play upon the surface of economic intercourse for the principles which work with silent, unperceived power. Accordingly in the following discussion I understand these concepts always in their most general significance.

(2) Revenue, according to this theory, includes all income which is derived, without one's own labour, solely from one's possessions. The existence of such an income in society no one will deny, even though it be asserted that this possession is the product of the possessor's own labour. To it belong rent of land, profits of capital, and interest on capital. Profits of capital and interest on capital are therefore no less revenue than the rent of land.

(3) As there can be no income which is not produced by labour, revenue depends upon two indispensable preliminary conditions. *First*, there can be no revenue unless labour produces at all events more than the labourers require in order to continue their work—for it is impossible for anyone not labouring himself to continue regularly to draw an income without such a surplus. *Secondly*, there can be no revenue if there be no arrangements which deprive the labourers of the whole or part of this surplus, and bestow it upon others who do not themselves labour; for by nature the labourers are the first to come into possession of their own productions. That labour yields such a surplus is due to economic causes, causes that increase the productivity of labour. That this surplus is in whole or in part taken away from the labourers and given to others is due to positive law, which has always allied itself to force, and which now effects this deprivation only by continued coercion.

(4) Originally it was slavery, whose beginning is coincident with that of agriculture and the ownership of land, which exercised this coercion. The labourers, who by their labour produced such a surplus, were slaves, and the master, to whom

the labourers and consequently the product also belonged, gave them only as much of it as was required for the continuance of their labour, keeping the rest or surplus for himself. When all the soil of a country has become private property, and all capital at the same time is in private possession, then the ownership of land and capital exercises a similar coercive power over freed or free labourers. For this ownership brings about, just as slavery did, that, *in the first place*, the product does not belong to the labourers but to the masters of land and capital; and *secondly*, that the labourers, possessing nothing, as against the masters who own the land and the capital, are glad to obtain out of the product of their own labour such a part as will suffice for their maintenance, that is, for the further continuance of their work. Thus the compact between the labourer and the master of wages has indeed taken the place of the slave-owner's orders, but this compact is free only in form not in reality, and hunger is an almost exact substitute for the lash. Only, that which was formerly called feed is now called wages.

(5) Revenue and wages are then the shares into which product, in so far as it forms income,

is divided. It follows hence that the greater the one share is, the smaller must the other be.* If revenue (rent of land and profits of capital combined) absorb a large share of the product, only a small one can be left over for wages. If the magnitude of one share changes, the other share must change inversely. As the magnitude of the shares in the product determines at the same time the *value* of the shares, the terms "high," and "rise," and "fall" are used to indicate the level and the changes of revenue and wages, these terms thus denoting relative conceptions. Revenue is said to be "high" or "rising," and wages "low" or "falling," when the former takes up a large or a growing share in the product, and the latter, consequently, a small or diminishing share in it.

(6) But in speaking of wages, the terms high and low level, rising and falling, are considered from another aspect besides. The degrading idea, namely, of "necessary wages" has been introduced into the science—of wages which comprise only

* From this point to 19, the relative change in wages and revenue will be considered under the supposition of *unchanged amount of labour* (*i.e.*, labouring population) and unchanged or changing productiveness; from 19 on, under the supposition of unchanged productiveness and changing amount of labour.

such an amount of commodities as is required by the workman to enable him to continue his work; thus the free labourer has again imperceptibly come to be regarded in the light of a slave who costs only as much in the way of sustenance as a machine does in repairs. This amount of necessary wages is taken as a criterion, as a fixed standard of measure, and wages are said to be high or rising, or, on the contrary, low or falling, according as they vary to the advantage or the disadvantage of the workmen by receding from or approaching that point. This conception of necessary wages does not, however, imply that actual wages cannot fall below that point, nor that it represents a quantity uniform at all times and in all countries.

(7) In dealing with the level or the change of wages, we must carefully distinguish between these two relations, which are by no means identical. In one relation wages may be high or be rising, while they may, at the same time, in reference to the other, be low or falling; and *vice versâ*. The creation of these effects depends entirely upon the degree or the change of the productiveness of labour. If, for example, the same amount of labour produces a large or a growing quantity of

commodities, then wages, considered as share of the product, may be low or be falling, while regarded in relation to the measure of necessary sustenance, they may be high or even rising. One ought to become familiar with the conception of both these movements of wages, for it may in future acquire a decisive influence in economic science and in the practical world.

(8) Originally the division of labour assumed such a shape that the masters of the land were also for the most part the masters of the capital. Capital comprises, logically—historically the scope of the concept has undergone great change, as has been shown in I.—raw materials, accessory materials, and tools; it is product which is used for future production; reduced to terms of labour, it is *stored-up labour*. As long as the masters of the soil are also masters of the capital the raw product will necessarily be developed, by slaves or free labourers, into the *finished product* in the same service, that of the landlords; the owner of land is at the same time the "manufacturer," and usually also the wholesale dealer in the finished wares. In such a condition the *entire revenue* will fall to the share of a single person, the owner of land and the owner of capital being merged into

one; and, in fact, there could be no recognized distinction between the revenue of land and the revenue of capital. This condition constituted the rule in ancient Greece and Rome, and is one of the reasons why the rich domain of political economy remained undiscovered by the ancients, and especially why they knew only money-capital, and did not even conceive of capital in its economic sense.*

(9) But if the division of labour has been so developed that land and capital have different owners, and that, therefore, the raw product which is produced by one set of workmen in the service of the landowners is then manufactured into finished wares by another set in the service of the capitalists, into whose possession this raw product is transferred; in that case the revenue will be divided, one part going to the owner of the raw product, the landowner, the other to the person who had this product converted into finished product, the capitalist. For if revenue in general originated, on the one hand, because labour produced *more* than was necessary for the

* See my paper, "Zur Geschichte der römischen Tributsteuern seit Augustus," in HILDEBRAND'S *Jahrbücher für Natrinalökonomie und Statistik*, vol. iv. *et seq*.

sustenance of the labourers, and, on the other, because positive law gave this surplus not to the labourers, but to the *owners* of the product of labour, there follows also the *division* of revenue—part of the product of labour which is in excess of that required for the labourers' maintenance going to *one* owner and part to *the other.* And it can make no difference that there exists this cross-wise division, as it were, of the products of labour between the two owners, the landlord and the capitalist, that in one and the same article the result of the work goes to the one in so far as it is raw product, to the other in so far as it is manufactured product, since the division takes place on the basis of value after all. Nor does the institution of private property produce a different effect upon the status of the labourers engaged in the production of raw materials or the labourers engaged in manufactures *after* its division into land and capital ownership from what it did *before* that division. With the German distinction between city and country, with the legal separation between "city trades" and agriculture, this separation between land ownership and capital ownership, and consequently the division of revenue into revenue of land and revenue of capital, first came into being as a thorough-going system, transforming the division of labour.

(10) This division is made according to the ratio which the *value* of the raw product bears to the *value* added to the raw product by the labour furnished by the capitalists in the way of manufacture or transportation*; in other words, in proportion to the fraction of the value of the finished product which is taken up by the raw product. The lower the value of the raw product in proportion to the value of the manufacture-product or *vice versa*, the smaller or the greater will be the part of the revenue falling to the raw product, the greater or smaller the part going to the manufacture-product.

(11) The owners of capital term the last part *profit of capital*, and *reckon* it according to the ratio it bears to the amount of capital; as has become customary, in comparison with a hundred or according to percentage. This ratio expresses the *rate* of the profit of capital. It sets the standard at the same time for the yield of the revenue of all applications of capital-property

* It is this added value, the addition accruing to the value of the raw material by the subsequent processes, that the author from this point on denotes by the word *Fabrikationsprodukt*, which I translate *manufacture-product.—Translator.*

[*Kapitalvermögen*]. People will not apply capital-property where it does not yield revenue in accordance with this standard; and as capital is required in the creation of raw product also, a part of the profit which falls to the raw product will have to be taken off as revenue or "*ordinary rate of profit,*" *reckoned by this standard,* upon the capital which has been invested. If there be a portion remaining beyond this, that portion is termed *rent of land,* because it falls to the owner of land purely as such, without regard to his being owner of capital or, it may be, labourer. And it is according to its rent that the value of a piece of land is estimated as capital or is "capitalized."

(12) As the profit on capital is greater the higher the percentage, it must rise or fall at the same rate as the ratio which the value of the raw product bears to the value of the manufacture-product. falls or rises. *For in the capital, upon which its share of the revenue which is called profit is reckoned by percentage, the value of the raw product is counted in, since the capitalists purchase it with their "capital-property."* Since now the revenue is divided according to the proportion which the value of the raw product bears to that

of the manufacture-product—so that if the latter is high a low value of the raw product must be reckoned in with the capital; and, on the contrary, if it is low a high value of the raw product is to be reckoned in with the capital—it is evident that the ratio of the profit on capital to the value of the capital (*i.e.*, the rate of interest) must rise with the rise of value of the manufacture-product or the fall of value of the raw product, and must fall in the opposite case. For the interest on capital (since the capitalist must buy the raw product) must be reckoned in the one case upon a relatively lower, and in the other upon a relatively higher capital-value.

(13) If the profit of capital is high, then the rent of land, so far as regards the division of the revenue, must be low. For if of that portion of the revenue—already a small one—which falls to the share of the landowner a still greater part has to be reckoned as profit on the capital he has applied, then a correspondingly smaller portion will be left over for the rent of land. Under such conditions, then, the profits on capital will swallow up the whole, or almost the whole, revenue of society, and can leave little or no remainder for

the rent of land. Yet the value of the raw product may easily be high enough to admit of a rent of land; rent must, for instance, always be left over where the value of the raw product is *equal* to that of the manufacture-product, and this for the reason that while in manufactures the value of the *material,* that is, the *whole of the raw product,* is reckoned in with the capital, in raw production it is the land itself which constitutes this material, and land does not come into play as capital. If in raw production land, regarded as material, were counted in with the capital, as is done, for instance, by purchasers* [or if in manufacture the raw product or material were not reckoned as capital, because it, too, belonged to the capitalists],† there could never be any rent of land left over, no matter how high the value of raw products might rise.

* Practical men who are not political economists dispute, therefore, that there is such a thing as rent of land at all; likewise acute jurists, as was shown in the discussion upon the principle of rent laid down by me.

† The passage enclosed between square brackets should be omitted in reading the sentence. What the author intended to say was, evidently, that if the material used in manufactures were not reckoned as capital, there would be rent in manufacture as there is in extractive industry; while if land were reckoned as capital, there would be no rent in extractive industry as there is none in manufacture. But, as it stands in the original, the sentence makes nonsense.—*Translator.*

(14) However, the *ratio of value between raw product and manufacture-product* can determine only the ratio of division between landlord and capitalist; can determine only in what ratio the whole revenue—the level of which is fixed by the ratio of division between it and wages—is to be further divided into rent of land and profit on capital. A variation in that ratio of value alone, therefore, merely takes from one part to give to the other. A rise in the value of raw product does, it is true, raise the rent of land, but only at the expense of the profit of capital which, on its side, must fall. A fall in the value of raw products does, it is true, raise the profits on capital, but only at the expense of the rent of land, which must now on its side fall. But no fall or rise in the value of raw product or of manufacture-product can in itself raise or lower the profit on capital, or raise or lower the rent of land, without effecting a contrary movement in the other part of revenue.

(15) A variation in one part of revenue which should *not* affect the other, or a variation in both parts of revenue in the same direction, as, for example, a rise in the rent of land without a fall in the profit on capital, or a rise both in rent

and in profit—the *shares in the product* only are here being considered throughout—can take place only if the ratio of division between wages and revenue varies, if revenue as a whole rises or falls. If, for instance, the revenue, which had amounted in value to $\frac{1}{4}$ of the product, $= x$, rose to $\frac{1}{2}$ of the product, $= 2x$, and if each part of revenue—rent of land and profit on capital—had before absorbed $\frac{x}{2}$ then, after this rise of revenue as a whole, one part of revenue could rise to $\frac{3x}{2}$ without the other having to fall, or they could both rise to x at the same time.

(16) It is clear that a simultaneous rise of both parts of revenue, rent of land and profit on capital, or the rise of one part which should not be at the expense of the other, must, since both can occur only in consequence of the rise of revenue as a whole, take place at the expense of the wages of labour. In this case wages must be limited to a smaller share of the product; they must vary inversely with the variation of one or both parts of revenue, and accordingly, in the above case, they must *fall.* Whether wages, which, to be sure, must fall *as share in the product*, fall as referred to the standard of the wages necessary

for subsistence, depends entirely upon whether at the same time the *productiveness of labour* has increased or not.

(17) If the productiveness of labour has not increased, and there is a rise either in one or in both parts of revenue, then wages must fall, whether regarded as share of the product or from the standpoint of the wages necessary for subsistence. For since, in this case, the product of a given amount of labour—the quantity of goods resulting from it—has not varied, a diminution in the proportional part, the share of the product, which anyone obtains must carry with it a diminution in the amount of product, the quantity of goods, which he receives. But suppose that the productiveness of labour has increased, that the same amount of labour produces more commodities, and that, accordingly, a greater quantity of commodities would fall to a given proportional part or share in the product going to the labourer. Then it still remains to be considered what relation the diminution of this proportional part, due to the rise of one or both parts of revenue, bears to the increase in productiveness or in the quantity of goods falling to a given proportional part. If, for instance,

productiveness has doubled, if, therefore, the product of a given amount of labour or a given proportional part of that product has doubled in amount—doubled in quantity of goods—wages as share of the product may diminish by a half, *e.g.*, from $\frac{1}{4}$ to $\frac{1}{8}$ of the product, while, measured by quantity of goods, or viewed in reference to the standard of "necessary wages," they have remained the same.

(18) In like manner a change in wages as share of the product must exert a contrary effect upon one or both parts of revenue. If a change has taken place in wages without an accompanying change in productiveness, then rent of land and profits of capital would benefit or suffer in the same proportion in which they have hitherto divided the revenue between them; for the ratio between raw product and manufacture-product can not on its part be changed by a change in wages unaccompanied by a simultaneous change in productiveness. If, however, the change in wages be accompanied by a change in productiveness, if, *e.g.*, wages have fallen while productiveness has increased, the question will be in what proportion extractive industry and manufactures have contributed to this increase in productiveness; and

that part of revenue whose productiveness has not increased, or has increased least, will alone or mainly profit by this rise—consequent upon the fall in wages—of the revenue as a whole.

(19) Up to this point only the effects of changes taking place in the various shares of the product, wages, rent, and profits, assuming either a constant or varying productiveness,* have been considered, without bringing in the question of a *change in the aggregate of the productive forces.* It still remains to note the effects of changes in the aggregate of the productive forces applied, which, in the last analysis, consist of changes in the quantity of labour, *i.e.*, the labouring population. Such a change in the aggregate of the productive

* Productive force and productiveness must be distinguished from each other. Productiveness signifies the efficacy or fruitfulness of productive force. If in place of ten labourers twenty labourers are employed, or in place of one machine of a given degree of efficacy two of the same kind are set up, the *productive force* has been doubled ; if ten labourers produce as much as hitherto twenty labourers, or if a machine has twice the efficacy of another machine involving the same expense, *productiveness* has doubled. Here, too, labour is the ultimate standard of measure. Greater quantities of labour are greater productive force ; more product with equal quantity of labour is increased productiveness. In recent times, owing to the more rapid increase of population and to industrial inventions, productive force has increased as well as productiveness, but their different effects have scarcely been regarded in political economy.

forces—leaving out of account any change in productiveness and any change in the ratio of division of the product between the labourers, the landowners, and the capitalists, changes only the aggregate of the national product; and thus, not exercising any influence upon the ratio of division, changes only the aggregate of wages and of both parts of revenue. There accrues, according as the productive forces have increased or diminished, *more or less* rent, there accrues *more or less* profit on capital. The individual wages alone remain constant. For since it is assumed that productiveness and the ratio of division of the product between the labourers, the landowners, and the capitalists, have remained constant, the additional product created by the increased labouring population is divided in the old way.

(20) However, the *increase* or *diminution* of revenue consequent upon the increase or diminution of the productive forces exercises an apparently different influence upon the rent of land from what it does upon the profits of capital. It *raises* or *lowers* the rate of rent, but not the rate of profit. *For the increased or diminished rent must always be reckoned upon the same quantity of surface*, since the land and individual parcels of

land do not grow, but are confined within fixed limits. The increased or diminished profit, on the contrary, is reckoned upon the increased or diminished capital, without which the assumed increase or decrease in the aggregate product cannot be conceived; the *rate of profit* cannot, therefore, rise or fall, but only a greater or less amount of profit accrue to the nation. While, then, the rent of a given piece of land may rise upon the same grounds upon which the profits of capital rise, namely, because revenue as a whole has risen at the expense of the labourer's share in the product, as well as because one part of revenue has risen at the expense of the other, rent may in addition rise from the third cause, the *increase* of the total revenue, while this does not occur in the case of profit. This last—to call attention already here to this point—is perhaps the most efficacious cause of the rise of rent, which circumstance, however, political economists have thus far not represented in a proper light, even though *Jones*, the chief opponent of Ricardo, alleges the augmentation of production to be one of the most important causes of the rise of rent.

(21) The legal regulation of property rights does not alter these principles of revenue. Rent of

land, *e.g.*, is merely *divided* between the higher and the lower landowner, the hereditary landlord, and the hereditary tenant-farmer, according to positive legal regulations. Just as little does the interpolation of the *entrepreneur* alter the above principles. The tenant-farmer only draws profit on his capital, and if he has made an advantageous lease, a part of the rent besides. The *entrepreneur* in the trades, in manufacture, and in transportation, in so far as he is distinguished from the capitalist, only divides the profits on capital with the latter, and that in accordance with the usual rate of interest on borrowed capital. But no regular gain upon enterprises can arise from anything but profits on capital —mortgage capital is not in question here, the interest on it being but an amount of *ground* rent, the loan on a piece of land but a purchase of rent—no regular profit on capital can arise from anything but revenue, no revenue from anything but the product of labour.*

(22) Within the circle of these numerous variations, then, may the division of the national

* Compare my pamphlet, *Für den Kredit der Grundbesitzer. Eine Bitte an die Reichstände.* Berlin, 1847. Since then I have written the more elaborate work upon the Principle of Revenue.

product revolve. Wages may vary as share in the product as well as in relation to the standard of necessary sustenance; equally in both respects, independently of each other, and even inversely; they may, *e.g.*, fall as share in the product, and yet rise in relation to necessary sustenance. If a fixed ratio of division be assumed between wages and revenue, then the two parts of revenue, rent and profit, can vary, as share in the product, only inversely; just as much as the one rises or falls must the other fall or rise. Again, if one part of revenue varies as share in the product without exercising any effect upon the other, or if both vary equally, this can only occur if a contrary variation takes place in wages; *e.g.* a rise in rent—as share in the product—without a fall in profit must lower wages as share in the product. An increase in revenue consequent upon the increase in the national product, however, raises rent also without lowering either the level of profit or wages as share in the product; and among the combinations, therefore, formed by these various changes the case is even conceivable where profit, wages—the latter likewise as share in the product—*and even rent* rise *simultaneously;* namely, when, though rent falls indeed as share in the product, and this fall accrues to the advantage of *both* the other shares, the relative fall is more than counterbalanced by the increase in the total revenue. One cannot pass a correct judgment upon the different phenomena of the division of the national product without being able to distinguish these points of view, to analyze these relations crossing and recrossing each other so variously, and thus to connect the individual phenomena with their peculiar causes.

(23) *If land and capital ownership exist in the society, and if the division of labour is left to itself, then the division of the national product takes place within this range of variation* [innerhalb dieser Wechselfälle] *in the form of* **exchange.** The individual exchange is made thus: A exchanges a product which is of less value to him—we mean here less value in use—for a product of B's which is of greater value to him. The same motive impels B. It is in this manner that the exchange of a certain *quantity* of both products is concluded. The *worth* which the one product as against the other acquires thereby, and which may be estimated by the quantity of the other obtained in exchange, is likewise termed value, *i.e.*, *exchange*

value. Exchange, therefore, proves to be a relation in which everyone produces value-in-use for another person, and obtains in consequence his compensation from that other person. And exchange value is nothing but value-in-use to others, which receives its compensation. Exchange value may, therefore, be also termed *social value-in-use;* that it is the former proves that it is the latter.

(24) The exchange value expresses at the same time the measure of compensation which the exchanger receives. *Assuming that each of the exchangers always produced exactly that quantity of value-in-use which the other requires to satisfy his successive needs, this compensation would be a just one only if it corresponded with the sacrifice, the cost, the amount of productive force which each exchanger has expended for the other in the production of the value-in-use.* Such would be the case if the product received in exchange contained a *like* sacrifice, an *equal amount of* cost, *the same* expenditure of productive force—in other words, if the exchange value coincided with the amount of cost, if in the products exchanged equal amounts of cost were exchanged. Labour is the original sacrifice, the primary cost, the

first and last productive force which is expended upon all products. *Under the above assumption* the exchange value of the products exchanged must be equal to the quantity of labour which has been expended upon them; in the exchange of products equal quantities of labour must always be exchanged for each other. And labour, varied as it is or appears to be in the various productions, does admit an *adjustment* and a *measure* according to the work and the time—days and the hours of labour.* But it is clear that if that assumption were not realized such compensation could make no pretension to justice; justice could not demand this rule of compensation. For if A has not produced the value-in-use required by B, if he has, consequently, expended uselessly a quantity of productive force, how can A demand compensation of B just as though he had realized that assumption? And this assumption will be least conformed to in isolated cases of exchange. Therefore the measure of compensation, the exchange value, will here depend upon the urgency of need and the supply of product of

* Compare the first paper in my work, *Zur Erkenntniss unsrer staatswirthschaftlichen Zustände*, etc. Also I. of the present work, where this is shown still more thoroughly.

each of the exchangers, *i.e.*, upon *individual demand and supply.* But even supposing that that assumption were realized, there would still have to be, since everything would depend upon human *knowledge* and human *will*, a just *estimate*, *adjustment*, and *determination* of the quantities of labour contained in the products to be exchanged; and for this purpose a *law* would be required to which the exchangers would submit.

(25) If exchange becomes the rule, because every participant produces now only value-in-use for others, social value-in-use, exchange value; because of the existence of the division of labour, that strong bond of union in which one works for all and all for one; exchange value becomes *market value.* In isolated, accidental cases of exchange the only exchange value that can come into question is that which one product received in exchange has as against another given in return; and this is controlled by *individual* demand and supply. The market value is the exchange value which each product has relative to *all* other products which are exchanged in commerce; and it is controlled by the *general demand and supply of the competitors.* The existence of market value is facilitated by the intervention of a peculiar

product, *a product intended for exchange alone*, a *market commodity* which is preferred to all others, and which, therefore, expresses the market value of all other commodities—the precious metals. Everybody first exchanges his product for this preferred market commodity, gold or silver, and only then exchanges the quantity which he has received of this commodity for that which he wishes to use. In ordinary life we say he *sells* and *buys;* exchange, then, resolves itself into two acts. Thus gold and silver perform the *office of money*, the conception of which is by no means that of a market commodity. The essence of money consists solely in its being a *certificate* of the market value which anyone has given away in his exchange-product, and which, in turn, he can realize as a *draft upon just the same amount of market value. Were it possible, therefore, to determine the market value according to the quantity of labour which the products have cost*, a money could be introduced which would answer perfectly to its conception. It would consist of strips of paper, which would constitute accurate *receipts* for the quantity of labour which each one had in trade delivered in his products, and therefore also *drafts* entitling him to obtain in trade the same quantity in return.* It is only a *historic* necessity, an *accident*, therefore, that till now money consists of a *commodity*, *i.e.*, is a certificate and a draft which expresses the value certified and drawn for always *by its own value.* It is well known that, because money is to-day a commodity which is itself, like all other products, subject to fluctuations in value, a given quantity of this money-commodity, or *an equal amount coined according to the same standard of coinage*, will after a time no longer represent the same value as before. And one can, therefore, in *this respect also speak*, *e.g.*, *of a rise in wages and in rent;* though not indeed of a rise in profit on capital, since the increased money-value of the income of capital is reckoned upon a like increased money-value of the capital, thus leaving the ratio between the two, which determines the level of profit, the same. Inasmuch as the quantities of the money-commodity are *coined* under certain *coin-names*, it may also happen that smaller quantities of money-commodity are substituted for the original ones; so that, finally, in this respect also a rise in wages and in rent, though

* Compare the last paper in my work, *Zur Erkenntniss unsrer staatswirthschaftlichen Zustände*, and I. of this work.

again not in profit, may take place. This is, indeed, a deception on the part of the administrators of the Mint, but it is one which it is well known has often been practised.

(26) Even though the market value, in a commerce left to itself, is subject to the changeful dominion of the general demand and supply, it *gravitates* at least towards the amount of productive force which has been expended in the creation of the product: towards its cost. It strives continually, at least, to allow a just compensation. For self-interest will, in competition, bring it about that no one will long obtain for a smaller amount of expended productive force a larger amount in the product he gets in exchange. For everybody would rush into such advantageous production until equilibrium would again be restored, and there would again be an equal expenditure of productive force, equal cost, equal labour in the products exchanged. But the actual movements of the market will nevertheless, like the oscillations of the pendulum, swing beyond this position of equilibrium on either side; though the school which has most closely followed in Adam Smith's footsteps, the school of Ricardo, takes this mere striving for the

accomplished fact itself, and bases all its further deductions, therefore, upon an assumption which does *not* exist in reality. That which *Ricardo* assumes to be realized is only what *should* take place, is one of the greatest, and practically also one of the most important of economic *ideas.* Just as in the theory of natural law the social contract was in the beginning regarded as an actual historical fact of the past, until a juster perception recognized in it only an *idea* according to which individual rights and duties should be regulated—a thing by its nature, therefore, to be realized in the future; so likewise the congruence of the exchange value of products with the quantity of labour which they cost is not a fact, but the grandest economic idea which has ever striven towards realization. That *law of gravitation*, however, to which allusion has been made accomplishes even to-day so much as this—that in general the market value of products is in inverse ratio to productiveness; that if with the same expenditure of productive force double the quantity of product is created, the market value of the original quantity of product will at the same time sink to half its former amount.

(27) Just as much market value as one has,

just so much *purchasing power* does he possess. Just as much purchasing power as one possesses, just so much value-in-use can he convert into market value through the process of exchange. In exchange, then, the value-in-use which every-one produces for society must have a correspond-ing purchasing power, otherwise it neither attains a market value in the hands of its producer, nor is of benefit to anybody in society, inasmuch as it does not command an equivalent. Producers can in exchange, therefore, produce only such a quantity of value-in-use as shall correspond to the actual purchasing power of society. While land and capital ownership exist the real pro-ducers, the labourers, have, indeed, no voice in the matter of the kind or the measure of pro-duction, for this depends entirely upon the will of the quasi-producers, the owners of the "production-fund" ["Productivfonds"]. In ex-change, then, the owners of the production-fund can make this fund effective only so far as the purchasing power of society compensates them for the products.

(28) Were the division of labour as simple a relation as political economists often represent it to be; did it, namely, assume the shape that

each participant produced a certain product entirely by and for himself, and consequently also reaped the proceeds of this product entirely himself; if, *e.g.*, A produced bread, B clothes, C shoes, D tables, and so on, and each one himself obtained the entire value of the product, then the purchasing power of each one would always be equal to the market value of his whole product. But the division of labour is not so simple as all that. The division is made not merely as those political economists assume, but in such a manner in addition that the owners of the production-fund, the landowners and capitalists, share with the real producers, the labourers, in every single product. For positive law declares land and capital to be as peculiarly the property of single individuals as labour-power [Arbeitskraft] is of the labourer. Consequently the labourers are compelled, in order to be able to produce at all, to enter into a combination with the owners of land and capital, and to share the product of labour with them. A false and superficial abstraction has, indeed, in *its* explanation of what landowners and capitalists receive in that compulsory division, pointed back to the special and varied services rendered to production by labour, land, and capital; and, again, has conceived the product created by this combination to be the result of these varied services operating together. But who does not see that this is the grossest *petitio principii* of which any science has ever been guilty, and, it may be added, the most pernicious practical error which still remains for the human understanding to combat! That combination certainly effects no alteration in the *natural* elements of the production of all commodities; it only removes a social hindrance to production, the arbitrary *Quod non* of the owners of land and capital, and removes this by a division of the **product.** Therefore, though it is true that under the form which the division of labour actually assumes to-day, there is still exchange of "products for products," as the economists express it, *yet the purchasing-power which each participant possesses is not, as those economists have further falsely concluded, regulated by the value of his product, but by his* **share in this product.** I beg my readers to consider this, that purchasing-power to-day is only *share in the product*, for to the fact that the Say-Bastiat school has overlooked this is it due that it so violently opposes the necessary further development of political economy.

(29) *In a society such as is here assumed and such as to-day still actually exists, the shares of the labourers, landowners, and capitalists in the product are not regulated by social foresight, by a* **rational** *social law, but are likewise left to be acted on by exchange left to itself; by the so-called* **natural** *laws of society.* It depends upon the chances of the market what the share of each class in the national product shall amount to. The relative shares of the landowners and the capitalists are, indeed, determined by the relative value of the raw product and the manufacture-product, and this gravitates, as has been shown, towards the cost of the respective products, or according to the law of the productiveness of the respective amounts of labour. Yet, because the *highest of economic goods*, the essence [Princip] of all products, *labour*, has also become an object of exchange, the more momentous division between revenue-receivers and labourers is given over to the domination of exchange. The labourer gives his labour in accordance with the laws of supply and demand to the *entrepreneur*, and receives for it, according to the same laws, its exchange value, his wages; *receives, therefore, his share in the product as determined by exchange.* A conception just as degrading as that

which gauged the wages of labour by the standard of necessary sustenance, or looked upon them in the light of machine repairs, is that which speaks of a "natural price" or "cost" of labour—labour, the essence of all commodities, regarded as itself a commodity—just as of the products of labour; and puts this natural price, this cost of labour, into the sum of the expenses that are necessary in order to keep up the supply of labour in the market, *i.e.*, in order to enable the labourer to reproduce his kind. What an absurd, indescribable contradiction in the conception of those economists who allow labourers in their legal status a voice in determining the destinies of society, yet at the same time want them to be treated economically only as commodities!—for *labour* in this connection is the *labourers.* Were the Say-Bastiat school self-conscious in all social relations, it would necessarily consist of census-takers only.

(30) *The division of the national product according to the "natural" laws of exchange has as its consequence that with increasing productiveness of labour the wages of the labourers become an always smaller share of the product.* For the labourers, even if they could perceive that by an altered combination of the same simple operations on

their part their labour grows always more productive, are economically not in a position to insist, as against their opponents in the bargain, that their labour should be compensated in exchange according to its productiveness, and according to the increase in that productiveness. With them the motives for exchange which determine them to get rid of their goods, namely labour, are of the most urgent nature, and thus is the highest of economic goods, the essence of all products, put on a level with a common and rather worthless commodity. The labourers own many hours of labour, but nothing more, and they have, therefore, fighting against them in the front rank, in exchange transactions, their own hunger and the sufferings of their families. Consequently they give away their labour easily, if only their most crying wants are satisfied by the exchange, if only this exchange amounts to enough to give them strength to continue their labour, *i.e.*, enable them by labour further to satisfy these crying wants. It is only when wages amount to still less —this is established by experience—when they are so low that the labourers in continuing their labour would do so at the expense of their bodily strength, only then do they desist from work, and rather steal, in accordance with a profound natural instinct that under such circumstances the moral conditions of social existence have been violated, and violated *against* them. But the *measure* of what satisfies those most crying wants is not a *quota* but a *quantity of product*, and a quantity which during a labourer's lifetime in the same country, and taking the average of the seasons, remains a pretty *constant quantity*. If labour, then, becomes more productive, if an equal quantity of labour creates more product, if, accordingly, an equal quantity of product represents a smaller quantity of labour, and, therefore, constitutes a smaller proportional share of the entire product, then it is evident, since those motives for exchange are dominant with the labourers, that with the increasing productivity of labour their wages become an always smaller quota of the product.

(31) In the development of society still other causes are added, which strengthen the labourers' motives to get rid of their product at "cost price." The more populous the country, the more productive its labour, and the greater at the same time the freedom of the individual, the more will the labourer, trade being left to itself, be forced to

work "cheap." For the more will labour be placed on a level with a commodity subject to the law of competition, and a competition which is harmful; and the more able will the *entrepreneurs* be to "give out" the work to those who demand the least. As if the *entrepreneurs* gave away the work instead of receiving it! But so perverted have even ordinary conceptions become in consequence of existing relations, that because to-day work cannot be done without *permission*, this permission is called the work itself. In the early conditions of modern colonies—which may be expressed by the formula: The arts and the capital of the old civilization, with entire political liberty, sparse population, and rich, superfluous land!—these laws keeping down wages appear, of course, to be changed; but their operations are only suspended, because here competition *for the time being* turns to the advantage of the labourers.* Under the conditions which exist in the mother countries where the decisive factor of that formula—fertile land more than sufficient for the population—is lacking; where the labouring classes have never occupied the position in which

* The *present* state of things in North America is a proof of this.

they are suddenly placed in the colonies; where, besides, released from the servile relations of centuries, they have carried with them into freedom the spirit of subservience and the habit of a merely necessary subsistence; where, when their emancipation took place, the conditions of population and of productivity were already against them*—there they are indeed no longer able to raise themselves by peaceful striving to a position from which they could successfully combat those laws. There want does not allow the spirit of freedom to nerve the moral force of these classes to the pitch of a firm determination to labour for such wages only as are worthy of a free citizen. There the full liberty of the labourer exercises an effect upon wages hardly different from that which easier means of transportation have upon the price of a commodity already depressed by competition; it only facilitates the *supply* of labour, only depresses the "price" of labour still more.

(32) *If every participant in exchange always retained the entire product of his labour, if his*

* England, in the last respect, forms an exception in Europe. There the labouring classes were already free before the English revolution, and they were, therefore, successful for a time in their struggles against those laws. That time, however, is long since past.

purchasing power, therefore, consisted in the market-value of the entire product—which, as is well known, the economists of the school of Ricardo, as of the Say-Bastiat school, falsely represent to be the case—*then no glut could arise from an increase of productiveness, either in respect to any* **one** *or to* **all** *commodities, until all the participants had received enough of them for their use, until more of them had been produced than is required by society.* For since the market value of the product is in inverse ratio to productivity, the market value of each man's product would remain constant, and consequently also his purchasing power; this as well in the case of those in respect to whose products there had been an increase in productiveness as of those who were not so placed. Every participant would be able to buy a larger quantity of every product in respect to which productiveness had increased; and the undiminished purchasing power of everyone could cope with the increased amount of product—consequent upon increased productiveness—until the wants of everyone were absolutely satisfied; until no one *would* buy more even though he *could.* In this case, then, the purchasing power of society would always remain commensurate with its productiveness; or, in other words, as much value-in-use as society might produce, so much market value and so much purchasing power would it possess also, until all the wants of every sharer in production were gratified; and value-in-use would cease to be market value and purchasing power only when it had itself ceased to be value-in-use any longer for anybody in society. As is familiar, the school of Ricardo and of Say endeavour also by this example to prove, *in the midst* of the woes of "overproduction," that no such thing can take place. And evidently this example also pictures the happiest economic outcome and condition that can possibly be imagined—a condition, namely, where there is overproduction only *after all* the members of society have fully satisfied their needs; while the commercial crises of to-day consist precisely in this, that simultaneously with superfluity, four-fifths or five-sixths of society suffer want. *A like success would attend the increase of productiveness even though the product were divided, as it is to-day, among three sharers, if* **the share of each one remained a fixed, unalterable quota of the product.** Under this supposition also the purchasing power of every participant in exchange would remain constant, be the increase in productiveness what it may. And overproduction in the case of one or of *all* commodities could likewise take place only after the needs of *all* the sharers were satisfied—even though, to reach that point, there would have to be, on account of that division of the product, a yet greater rise in productiveness than in the condition assumed by Ricardo and Say, where each one would have the market value of his entire product at his disposal. *But if neither of these assumptions is realized, if the product is not only divided among three sharers, but the share of the labouring classes (i.e., of the great majority of society) is besides, in accordance with the "natural" laws of trade left to itself, not a fixed, unalterable quota of the product* **but, on the contrary, becomes a smaller quota of the product exactly in proportion to the increase in productiveness**—*then that fortunate issue of the increase in productiveness cannot occur.* For according to this third supposition, purchasing power and productiveness are no longer in direct proportion to each other. On the contrary, the purchasing power of the greatest part of society diminishes in proportion to increasing productiveness; and society is placed in the position of producing value-in-use which is no longer market value and purchasing power, while yet the need for it is, in the case of most people, unsatisfied.

(33) It is obvious that wherever and whenever the "*natural*" laws of trade produce such effects, and no *rational* laws interpose a dam against those effects, phenomena must necessarily occur in consequence, which resemble those that are to-day called gluts and pauperism. A phenomenon *must* necessarily then arise as irrational as this: that the productiveness of society may rise ever so high, may rise so very high that *all* its members *could* live in affluence from its proceeds, and yet, and even because of that very productiveness, the majority are thrown into poverty, and the minority into loss of property. In virtue of the connection of economic development with legal and political development, which on its part carries with it an always greater degree of legal equality and political freedom, the fatal contradiction *must* then be generated in society that the greater the equality and freedom of its members legally and politically, the more unequal and dependent does the condition of the *majority*, the labouring classes, become. For as regards *commercial crises*, overproduction must take place

before the needs of society are fully satisfied, since the purchasing power of the majority of society, of the working classes, diminishes in proportion to the increase of productiveness. And as regards *pauperism*—since the material demands of the majority of society, the labouring classes, are constantly rising, and their desires are constantly inflamed by seeing the wealth of the minority alone increase, while the measure of their income diminishes, or remains the same, and therefore at least relatively diminishes—the economic position of the labouring classes must necessarily be a distracted one. In a word, the result must be the incredible absurdity that though the majority of society are languishing in poverty, they cannot by far put their productive force into full activity, since then even the smaller portion would also be plunged into poverty.

(34) In these "natural" laws of exchange left to itself lies the key to the economic problems of the present time. *The assumptions from which such phenomena as pauperism and commercial crises have just been deduced as necessary conclusions, actually exist to-day; and society has thus far promulgated no laws to check the consequences, now also growing practical, of assumptions which*

have become practical. Productiveness has in fact greatly increased, and though the increase has been far greater in manufacture and transportation than in the production of raw material, the increase in the last, too, has been considerable. The national product has, moreover, been largely increased also through the increase in productive *force* consequent upon the growth of population. Wages in Europe, on the other hand—where they have never been favoured by colonial conditions such as prevail in North America and Australia, but have been evolved, under the conditions of far greater density of population and of land already fully occupied, from the wage-relations of serfs—have never in general risen much or for any length of time above the point of necessary wants. Other social circumstances have besides developed in such a way that they have exerted a constantly depressing effect upon them. And accordingly the consequences, the present form of division of the national product, have been inevitable. Wages in Europe have in fact become an always smaller share of the product. In consequence of this, revenue as a whole has risen, and this rise has mainly benefited rent, since productiveness has increased more in manufacture and transportation than in the production of raw materials; it has directly benefited profit on capital only in so far that without this rise in revenue as a whole it would have fallen still lower. The rent of one and the same piece of land has in addition experienced a considerable rise through *the increase of revenue* consequent upon the increase of productive force, and it is this in great part which has raised it to its present high level.* This form of division of the national product, then, has decreed against society pauperism and commercial crises. They have both become facts, as fully as that division and the assumptions from which they were deduced. There is no longer an optimism so blind or a self-interest so narrow as not to acknowledge the existence of phenomena which have sprung into life with such violence, and which arouse such general attention. Those who still deny them no longer count. The controversy no longer turns upon the existence of these

* The landowners, in spite of this, do not grow rich; for with the freedom of the ownership of land, and the mortgaging of it in the shape of negotiable capital, landed property is always involved in debt to its full value, and passes into the hands of the capitalists. See my work, *Zur Erklärung und Abhilfe der heutigen Creditnoth des Grundbesitzes.* Jena, Fr. Mauke, 1869.

phenomena, but upon the means of remedying them; or at most upon the assertion of their absolute necessity by that little group which is in the habit of regarding social perversities as the "will of God."

Those assumptions will in reality reach out still farther. Since the various industries have allied themselves with the progress of the natural sciences, the increase in productiveness is incalculable. Chemistry and mechanics make man by degrees a new creator, with the calling and the desire to supplement Nature wherever she is inadequate. Only one thing may be foreseen in this undoubted further increase in productiveness: the increase in extractive industry, especially in food products, will in the future no longer lag behind that in the productiveness of manufacture and transportation. Husbandry has not thus far drawn marked advantage from the advances in either chemistry or mechanics. It is to-day but little more than technology was only a few decades ago, little more than crude empiricism. In our day agricultural chemistry is only beginning to open up prospects which, though they will doubtless lead to many a false path, will finally put the creation of food products as completely in the power of society as it is in its power to-day to supply any desired quantity of cloth, provided only there be the necessary provision of wool. And yet if no rational laws oppose the "natural" ones, pauperism and commercial crises will continue to be the companions of reality, and society will continue to be in possession of productive forces whose efficacy could be of avail to all, but which cannot be allowed to become effective lest they be harmful to all. Will society suffer this? Will a school, undoubtedly ardent for liberty, succeed in inoculating society itself with their own confusion of "creation" and history, of *nature* and *society?* I doubt it! *In nature alone do things and relations contain their own rational law within themselves; in society they demand this of man.* And necessity will help to lead *society* to a recognition of this truth, if doctrine alone should not suffice.

This, then, is the theory, my honoured friend, which I oppose to yours, and which I will likewise briefly review.

To the labour of society I join a productiveness which has increased in great degree in all branches of industry, and particularly also in all branches of agriculture, and whose further increase is unlimited. But the "*natural*" laws which, in a commerce left to itself, where land and capital ownership exist, govern the division of the social product, prevent that increase from proving an unalloyed blessing to society. For on the one hand, they cause this division to assume the form of *exchange*, in which the private owners of the landed and capital property of society can institute no production at all, or none beyond the capacity of the existing purchasing power; and on the other hand, they not only cause the product to be divided between these owners and the labouring classes, but also bring it about that *the share of the latter in the product, and therefore the purchasing power of the majority of society, grows always smaller.* They produce this last effect because labour, the creator of all product, becomes likewise a commodity which is paid —*i.e.*, is recompensed, or receives its share of the product—according to the laws of supply and demand; and because these laws, in the development of society, prove, precisely with growing productiveness, increasingly disadvantageous to those who possess this "commodity," *i.e.*, to the labouring classes.

Thus, because according to the "natural" laws of trade the productive force of society can manifest itself only to the extent to which there is a corresponding purchasing power, and the same laws, again, with increasing productiveness lower the purchasing power of the majority, the effect of these laws is that an increase of fortune which should by its nature serve only the growth of the well-being and happiness of society becomes a cause of the opposite. The increase in productiveness which should make all richer, only causes, according to the "natural" laws of trade, one part of society to grow poorer, while it injures and jeopardises even the prosperity of the other, the favoured part.

These "natural" laws have the effect, then, that productiveness to-day can never manifest itself to a degree corresponding to its real capacity. Though ever striving to do so, it is crippled by commercial crises, and is forced to lie fallow, while it is capable of bearing fruit adequate for all the members of society who are languishing in poverty. The calculation, therefore, that if the present national income were distributed equally among all the individuals of society the sum falling to each would still be inconsiderable, is a false one. For the gain that would result from a distribution which would allow a full manifestation of the productive forces of society ought manifestly to be included in the computation.

Thus the "natural" laws of trade have plunged society into a direful contradiction; have cast an evil spell, as it were, over it. Under the form which the division of labour and the division of the national product have assumed, production can advance in proportion to productiveness only if the ratio of division of the product between the owners of the production-fund and the labourers is at least a constant one, or one that varies to the advantage of the latter. But the "natural" laws of that form have as a consequence that this ratio is not constant, but one that varies to the detriment of the labouring classes. *Production*, with trade left to itself, can prove beneficial to society only if *distribution* is good, and the laws of trade left to itself as regards distribution have precisely the consequence that distribution is necessarily bad.

What, then, should society do? She must step out of this fatal circle, in which she is driven about by prejudices alone, and replace the "natural" laws, in so far as they are harmful, by rational ones! For this she needs but clear vision and moral strength! It is the part of political economists to sharpen the first. Should the last be lacking for a free resolve, history will indeed have to swing the lash of revolution over her again.

I have thus far, my honoured friend, purposely confined myself to an abstract, methodical form, for it is possible that these letters may fall into the hands of one or other of the "learned" German economists, and they are not accustomed to any other treatment of our science. In my third letter, in which I shall endeavour to refute your views and to establish mine more in detail, I shall strive to be more popular. Perhaps one form will aid the other, to the better understanding of the unusual economic conceptions contained in them.